Zoe in Barcelona

A sapphic love story

Necool

Published by Franklin Publishers
Printed in the United States of America

For permissions, inquiries, or additional copies, contact:
Franklin Publishers
www.franklinpublishers.com

I knew I'd never be the same
Yet I loved hard anyways - Necool

Chapters

Chapter 1

New Beginnings

It was early December 2023. The sun was dipping below the horizon, casting an orange glow over the city as Ellie's SUV pulled up to the curb. The back was packed with boxes, and her dog, Maxie, was panting happily in the passenger seat. She looked up at the apartment building, a sense of relief washing over her. A new start, she thought.

Zoe was already inside, unpacking her life into the sprawling apartment they'd decided to share. The sound of clinking glasses and soft humming filled the air as Ellie walked in, Max's tags jingling with each step.

"This place is amazing, Zoe," Ellie said, looking around at the high ceilings and exposed brick.

Zoe smiled, wiping her hands on her jeans. "It's not bad for a fresh start. I even found the perfect spot for your piano."

Ellie raised an eyebrow. "Oh, yeah? And where's that?"

Zoe led her to a large window overlooking the city skyline. "Here. You can play while the sun sets. It'll be inspirational."

Ellie laughed, pulling Zoe into a tight hug. "You're the best, you know that? Thanks for doing this with me."

"Hey, what are besties for?" Zoe replied, hugging her back. And look, we even have our own fireplace. How fucking cozy is that?"

The intercom buzzed, and Kris's voice filled the room. "Hello, my lovely ladies! I come bearing housewarming gifts and champagne!"

Ellie buzzed him in, and soon Kris was sweeping into the room, a bundle of energy and laughter. He handed each of them a small potted plant. "A little something from Chloe's shop. She said they're supposed to bring good luck and new beginnings."

"That was sweet of her," Zoe said, setting her plant on the kitchen counter.

Kris popped the champagne and poured them each a glass. "To new beginnings," he toasted.

"To new beginnings," Ellie and Zoe echoed, clinking glasses.

The night was filled with laughter, stories, and a few tears as they reminisced about old loves and recent experiences. Gosh, they talked about everything and nothing, the conversation flowing as freely as the wine. Zoe and Ellie shared their plans for the future—focusing on themselves, learning boundaries, stop fucking people pleasing, and eventually dipping their toes back into the dating pool.

Kris finally said his goodbyes, leaving Ellie and Zoe alone in their new home.

They stood side by side, looking out at the city lights, a comfortable silence between them. Then, softly, Zoe began to sing. It will soon become a favorite to sing together, "Birds of a Feather" by Billie Eilish.

When Zoe finished, Ellie slipped an arm around her waist. "That was beautiful, Zoe. You're going to do amazing things, you know that?"

Zoe leaned her head on Ellie's shoulder. "We both are, El. We've been through the darkness, and now it's time to shine."

And so, in that moment, under the city lights, Ellie and Zoe took their first steps towards becoming the best versions of themselves, ready to face whatever the world might throw at them. Their journey was just beginning, and neither could predict the twists and turns, the loves and losses, that lay ahead. But they knew one thing for certain - they would face it all together.

As they drifted off to sleep in their new rooms, the embers in the fireplace cast a warm glow over the apartment. The city lights twinkled outside their windows, a beacon of the adventures yet to come. And so, their story began, filled with hope, love, and the promise of a future waiting to be written.

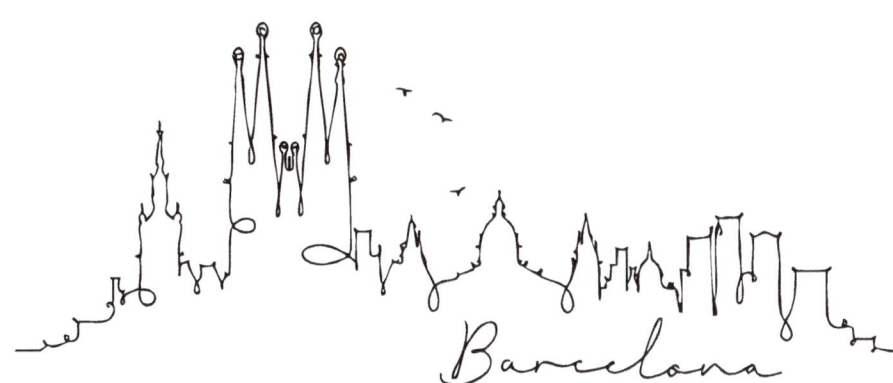

Chapter 2

Comfort Zones

The first few weeks in their new apartment were a whirlwind of unpacking, decorating, and exploring the city. Ellie and Zoe found themselves falling into a comfortable rhythm, their days filled with work and their nights with each other's company. They'd cook dinner together, laughing and chatting about their days, and then curl up on the couch with a bowl of Zoe's famous popcorn & wine, Maxie snoring softly at their feet.

The apartment became their sanctuary, a safe space where they could be utterly themselves. They'd dance around in their bras, sing at the top of their lungs, and talk about everything under the sun. It was more than they'd expected, this sense of comfort and belonging. It was healing.

Yet, with the new year approaching, they both felt a tug towards their pasts. Late one night, Zoe found herself staring at her phone, her ex's name glowing on the screen. She missed the familiarity, the comfort of the known. Across the hall, Ellie was doing the same, her finger hovering over the last messages read.

The next morning, they confessed their near-relapses over coffee.

"I texted her again last night," Zoe admitted, her voice barely above a whisper.

Ellie sighed, "Me too, but I didn't respond when she texted about missing me. I don't know what's wrong with me. Her & I are not meant to be, and I know that. I shouldn't talk to her and confuse us both again if we are broken up."

Zoe reached across the table, squeezing Ellie's hand. "There's nothing wrong with you, El. It's normal to miss what we had. But we have to remember why we left. We deserve better."

Ellie nodded, determination in her eyes. "You're right. We fucking do."

As the countdown to the new year began, they made a pact. No more looking back. No more *almosts*. They were going to break their patterns, step out of their comfort zones, and embrace the unknown.

New Year's Eve found them on the rooftop of their building, listening to Fred Again on repeat, watching the city sparkle below. As the clock struck midnight, they clinked glasses, their laughter echoing in the cold night air.

"To new adventures," Ellie toasted.

"To hot women and badass queens," Zoe added, a wicked grin on her face.

They drank, their eyes scanning the city, their hearts open and ready. The past was behind them, and the future was a sea of possibilities. They were single, independent, and fucking fabulous. And they were ready to take on the world, one hot woman at a time.

As they went to bed that night, the city still buzzing with celebration, they knew that 2024 was going to be their year. It was time to let go of the past for good and step into their power. And they were ready. Girl, were they ready.

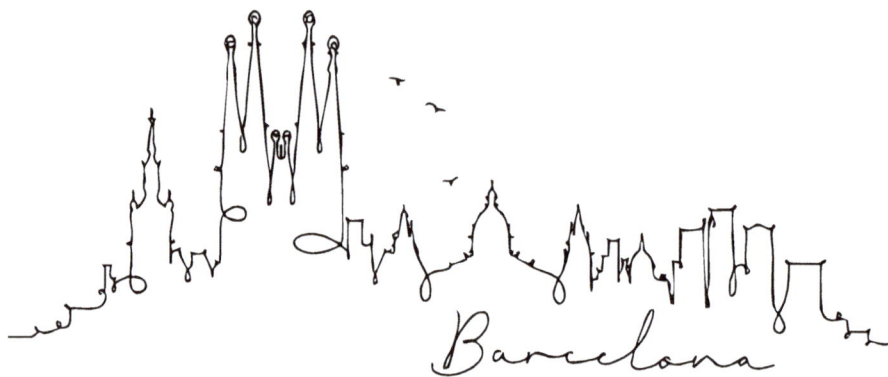

Chapter 3

The Canvas of Uncertainty

———◦♥◦———

Z oe woke up to the sound of her alarm, the familiar beep echoing through her room. She rolled over, her hand smacking the nightstand as she searched for her phone. She squinted at the screen, her eyes adjusting to the bright light. Ten emails, five messages, and a reminder. Her reminder. Today was the day she officially became unemployed.

The hotel she'd managed for the past six years was being sold, the new owners planning to convert it into a series of Airbnbs. She'd known it was coming had she watched the slow decline of the once-thriving business. But instead of dread, she felt a spark of excitement. This was her chance to finally take a breath, to step back and reassess her life.

She padded into the kitchen, the smell of coffee already filling the air. Ellie was leaning against the counter, her eyes scanning her laptop screen. She looked up as Zoe entered, a grin spreading across her face.

"So, today's the day, huh?" Ellie asked, handing Zoe a steaming mug.

Zoe smiled, taking a sip. "Yep. It's official. I am jobless." Ellie chuckled, "And yet, you're strangely happy about it."

Zoe leaned against the counter, her mind whirring. "I am. I mean, I loved that job, but it was also...safe. Predictable. I think it's time for something new." Ellie raised an eyebrow, "Any ideas?"

Zoe shrugged, "Not a clue. But I have some savings, so I'm not in a rush. I wanna take some time, cross off some bucket list concerts, visit my family, see some friends. Maybe travel a bit."

Ellie nodded, her eyes thoughtful. "You know, this could be your chance to tap back into your artistic side. Remember those songs you used to write?"

Zoe laughed, "God, they were sappy huh?."

Ellie shook her head, "They weren't. They were raw and real. And your photography...you've always had this way of capturing emotion. Maybe it's time to explore that again."

Zoe looked down at her coffee, her mind drifting. She remembered the headphones always on her ears listening to instrumental, the way words would flow from her pen. She remembered the darkroom, the smell of chemicals, the thrill of watching an image appear on a blank page.

"Maybe," she said, looking up at Ellie. "I don't know what I want, but I'm open to anything. I just want to feel...alive."

Ellie smiled, clinking her mug against Zoe's. "Then here's to new beginnings, to uncertainty, and to feeling fucking alive."

Zoe grinned, taking a sip of her coffee. She didn't know what the future held, but she was ready to dive in, ready to paint her life onto the canvas of uncertainty. Little did she know, the canvas was far bigger than she imagined, filled with colors she'd never seen, and a figure waiting in the wings. A figure named Sofia, standing on the cobblestone streets of Europe. But that was a story yet to unfold, a song yet to be written. For now, Zoe was content to stand at the edge, her heart open, her eyes scanning the horizon, ready for whatever came next.

As the days turned into weeks, Zoe found herself in a rhythm. She spent her mornings writing, her afternoons exploring the city with her camera, and her evenings with Ellie, laughing and planning. Chloe came over a lot to visit Ellie. They've been friends for 4 years but have recently been getting closer. Secretly crushing on each other. Chloe always brings them flowers cause she's an amazing florist with a little shop called The Prim Rose they love to support! In exchange, Zoe would cook for them or make watermelon spicy margaritas!

Zoe also got to see her other friends she loved and adored, Kris, who is mutually Zoe and Ellie's guy best friend! Charlie & Leo, Parker & London, who are obviously the hottest gay guy couples in the city, and of course, wild Annabella, who visits her a few times a year. Poor thing, she's stuck in Kansas, or wait, is it Kansas City, Missouri? Zoe, Always forget.

Zoe makes plans to visit her family soon. She reconnected with old friends and caught them up on what seemed like years went by before she had a chance to really have quality time.

But life, as Zoe knew all too well, was a mixture of light and dark. And as she stepped into her newfound freedom, she braced herself for the inevitable storm, unaware that it was already brewing, ready to shake her to her core. But that was a tale for another day. For now, she danced in the sunlight, her heart light, her spirit free, her canvas waiting to be filled.

Chapter 4

Shadows and Light

⸻ ♥ ⸻

The sun streamed through the window, casting a warm glow over Zoe's room. It was a Saturday morning, and she had planned to spend the day exploring the city with Ellie, but her heart felt heavy as if it were tethered to a weight she couldn't shake off. The past few weeks had been a whirlwind of emotions, and she had been riding the highs of newfound freedom while simultaneously grappling with the looming shadow of her father's illness.

Zoe took a deep breath, trying to gather her thoughts. Her phone buzzed on the nightstand, and she reached for it, glancing at the screen. It was a text from her sister, Mia.

"Hey, just checking in. How's your day going? Love you."

Zoe smiled softly, her heart aching at the thought of her sister. They had always been close, but the recent events had brought them even closer. They were navigating the storm together, united in their love for their father.

"Love you too. Just waking up. Let's catch up later?" Zoe replied, setting the phone down and staring out the window.

Her father had always been her greatest supporter, the one who encouraged her to chase her dreams without fear. He had been her rock, the one who filled her life with laughter and wisdom. But now, the news of his stage four cancer had turned their world upside down. The doctors had given him little time, and the family had decided to bring him to the city where Zoe and Mia lived, opting for home hospice care.

In April, when he had moved in, Zoe had been filled with hope. She wanted to make the most of every moment, to create memories that would last a lifetime. But within weeks, the reality of his condition became clearer. The vibrant man who had once brought so much joy into their lives was fading, and with each passing day, Zoe felt a piece of her heartbreak.

She remembered the last visit they had together before he moved. They had spent the day in the park, laughing and reminiscing about old times. He had told her stories of his youth, tales of adventure and when he fell in love with her mom that made her feel connected to him in a way that transcended time. But beneath the laughter, Zoe had sensed a shift, a fragility that hadn't been there before.

She recalled the day the doctor had delivered the news. The sterile room, the clinical terms, and the way her father had held her hand, his grip strong yet trembling. "Zoe, it's okay," he had said softly, his voice steady. "I've had a good long life. You and Mia are my greatest achievements. I'm so proud of you both. Just promise me you'll live. Don't let this stop you from chasing your dreams."

Those words echoed in her mind, a haunting reminder of the promise she had made. She wanted to honor him, to live fully, but the pain of his impending loss loomed over her like a dark cloud.

As the days passed, she spent as much time as possible with him, sitting by his bedside, sharing stories, laughter, and tears. On May 2nd, the day they held his hand as he slipped away, Zoe felt as if she had lost a part of herself. The room had been filled with a profound silence, the kind that wraps around you, heavy and still. She had watched as he took his last breath, a moment that felt both surreal and painfully real.

The funeral had been filled with beautiful condolences, a whirlwind of grief that left her feeling lost. But amidst the sorrow, she had found solace in the memories they had created together. She could hear his laughter, see his smile, and feel the warmth of his embrace, and in those moments, she knew he was still with her.

After the funeral, as she sat on the couch with Mia, the weight of their loss felt unbearable. They shared stories about their father, recounting the moments that had shaped their lives. "He always wanted us to be happy," Mia said, her voice thick with emotion. "He believed in us, Zoe. He wanted us to live."

Zoe nodded, tears streaming down her face. "I know. I just... I don't want to forget him. I don't want to let the sadness take over."

Mia wrapped her arms around her sister, holding her tightly. "We won't forget him. He lives on in us, in everything we do. We have to keep his spirit alive."

In that moment, Zoe realized that her father's legacy was not just in the memories they had shared, but in the way he had taught them to embrace life. He had always told them not to stress, to find joy in the little things, and to chase their dreams with fervor.

With a newfound resolve, Zoe wiped her tears and took a deep breath. "You're right. He wouldn't want us to dwell in sadness. He'd want us to celebrate life. To you, Dad, to celebrating your life."

Mia smiled through her tears, and together, they made a pact to honor their father's memory by living fully, by embracing the uncertainty of life and all the beauty it had to offer.

As the weeks turned into months, Zoe began to explore her passions again. She started writing songs, pouring her heart into every lyric, allowing the pain to transform into something beautiful. She picked up her camera, capturing moments that reminded her of her father's love for life. Each click of the shutter felt like a tribute to him, a way to keep his spirit alive in the world. She went to see her favorite bands in concert. Fred Again, of course, was one of them. It was a huge part of her healing process to see that show live and cry in happiness. Tribute to Dad as well! Music was always so important to her soul. She went on a few road trips and train rides. Basically trying to remember to explore things that made her happy.

Zoe also found herself leaning on Ellie more than ever. They spent countless evenings together, sharing wine and laughter, their friendship deepening as they navigated their own paths of healing.

Ellie had lost her father about a year ago from Cancer as well. So, if anyone understood Zoe's pain, reality, experience, and struggle right now, it would be Ellie. Just yet another thing they bounded over this year. Ellie became a source of strength for Zoe, encouraging her to embrace her artistry and reminding her that it was okay to feel, to grieve, and to celebrate all at once.

One evening, as they sat on the couch, Zoe turned to Ellie, her heart full. "I want to do something special for my dad. Something that honors his memory."

Ellie nodded, her eyes bright with understanding. "What do you have in mind?"

Zoe bit her lip, her mind racing with possibilities. "I want to host a small gathering, invite family and friends, and share stories about him. Maybe we can even have an open mic where people can share their favorite memories or sing songs that remind them of him."

"That sounds beautiful," Ellie said, her voice warm. "He would love that. It's a perfect way to celebrate his life."

And so, Zoe began to plan the gathering, pouring her heart into every detail. She created a playlist of songs that reminded her of her father, decorated the apartment with flowers and candles, and reached out to friends and family, inviting them to join in this celebration of life.

On the day of the gathering, Zoe felt a mix of excitement and nervousness. Each person brought their own stories, their own memories, and as they shared, Zoe felt her father's presence in the room, a comforting embrace that wrapped around her heart.

As the night unfolded, Zoe stood up, her heart racing. "I want to share something," she said, her voice steady despite the emotions swirling within her. "My dad taught me so much about life, about love, and about chasing dreams. He always believed in me, and I want to honor that belief by living fully by embracing every moment. So tonight, let's celebrate him together."

With that, she asked Ellie to start playing the piano, and As Ellie hit the first chord of a song she had written in his memory, "My King," she felt the tears streaming down her face, but they were no longer tears of sorrow. They were tears of love, of gratitude, and of hope.

As she sang, the room fell silent, each voice joining hers in harmony, a tapestry of memories woven together in a beautiful tribute. In that moment, Zoe knew that her father would always be with her, guiding her, cheering her on, and reminding her to live, to love, and to embrace the light that comes after the shadows.

Chapter 5

Summer of Connections

———❤———

June arrived with a burst of color and warmth, the kind that wrapped around the city like a vibrant embrace. Zoe stepped outside, the sun kissing her skin, and she felt a flicker of excitement. After the heavy months of grief and reflection, the arrival of summer felt like a promise—a chance for renewal, for laughter, and for new connections. The air buzzed with anticipation as the city prepared for its annual Pride celebrations, a month dedicated to love and acceptance, a celebration of identity that had always held a special place in Zoe's heart.

"Can you believe it's almost Pride?" Ellie exclaimed as she joined Zoe on the balcony, a mug of steaming coffee in hand. Her hair was pulled back in a carefree ponytail, and her eyes sparkled with enthusiasm. "We need to make this summer unforgettable!"

Zoe laughed, the sound bubbling up from her chest. "I'm all for unforgettable. But what exactly do you have in mind?"

Ellie leaned against the railing, her gaze fixed on the bustling street below. "I think it's time we both start dating again. Seriously, we've been through so much, and it's time to embrace life. What do you say?"

Zoe felt a familiar flutter of anxiety at the thought. "Dating? Like... dating apps and everything? You know how I feel about those."

"Exactly! That's the challenge! We can't let our past experiences hold us back. Besides, I'm determined to dive into the dating pool headfirst. You should join me!" Ellie's enthusiasm was infectious, and Zoe couldn't help but smile at her friend's unyielding spirit.

"Okay, okay," Zoe relented, though a part of her still felt hesitant. "But you know I'm not great at this whole dating thing. What if I embarrass myself?"

"Who cares? We're all about celebrating our true selves this summer! Let's make it fun! We can share our stories and laugh about epic fails. It's going to be hilarious!" Ellie's laughter rang out, and Zoe found herself caught up in the excitement.

"Fine," Zoe said, rolling her eyes playfully. "But if we're doing this, we need a system. Or I'll start mixing them up. Can you imagine? Umm, Ellie, how was last night? Was it clingy blonde or recently divorced chic, or what's her name, the polyamorous one again?"

Ellie grinned, her eyes glinting with mischief. "A joint calendar! We'll code the names so only we understand who's who. It'll be our secret code for dating. And trust me, it will be hilarious to look back on."

With that, Zoe felt a flicker of hope. Maybe this summer could indeed be different. As the days passed, she and Ellie dove into the world of dating apps, swiping through profiles and laughing at the absurdity of some of the bios. Zoe found herself surprised by how many women shared her interests— music, art, and a love for adventure. It felt like a treasure trove of possibilities, and she began to feel a sense of excitement about what lay ahead.

Ellie took the lead, and soon, she was juggling multiple conversations with women she'd met online. "You won't believe this," she said one evening, her eyes wide with excitement. "I have a date with three different women this week!"

Zoe raised an eyebrow, half-amused and half-concerned. "Three? At the same time?"

Ellie shrugged, her grin unabashed. "Why not? It's like speed dating but in my own style! I'll figure out who I click with best and go from there. Plus, it's just practice, right?"

Zoe couldn't help but laugh. "You're going to need a spreadsheet to keep track of everyone!"

"Exactly! It's a dating buffet, Zoe! You can take a little bit of everything until you find what you like!" Ellie's enthusiasm was contagious, and Zoe felt her own apprehensions begin to fade.

Zoe grinned, feeling a sense of camaraderie with her friend. "I guess we're both in this together, huh? Dating is a wild ride."

"Absolutely! And just think, Pride is right around the corner. We'll have so many stories to share by then!" Ellie's eyes gleamed with excitement. They broke into a random dance in the living room before breaking off into their rooms.

As the summer days unfolded, Zoe and Ellie continued to navigate their dating escapades, each encounter bringing laughter, confusion, and unexpected connections. They embraced the chaos, the thrill of meeting new people, and the joy of discovering themselves in the process.

After several dates with beautiful random women, Ellie also starts to date her friend Chole, remembering her as the florist! She started at first, coming over and joining Ellie and Zoe on the nights out, all being single and playing wingman for one another. Then one night after the bar closed and we walked home laughing and singing, Chloe turned to Ellie and said, "You're so fucking cute, I wanna kiss you." Chloe locks eyes with Ellie and then intensely directs her stare at her big, beautiful lips. That night, they hooked up, and before you knew it, Chloe was part of the queue of women, too. Chloe and Ellie started dating but also they were both still dating other people.

Chapter 6

House of Queens & Love

⎯⎯♡♥♡⎯⎯

The scent of fresh flowers filled the air as Chloe entered the apartment, her arms laden with bouquets. Ellie rushed to greet her, her eyes lighting up at the sight of the vibrant blooms. "You spoil us, Chloe," Ellie said, taking the flowers and setting them on the kitchen counter.

Chloe smiled, her eyes soft. "Only the best for my queen." She leaned in, planting a soft kiss on Ellie's lips, a kiss that lingered and deepened, sending a shiver down Ellie's spine.

Over the past few weeks, Ellie and Chloe's relationship had blossomed into something neither of them had expected. What started as a casual fling had turned into a deep, passionate connection. They found themselves drawn to each other in a way that made every other date pale in comparison. They decided to commit to each other, choosing to explore the depths of their love without the distractions of other women.

Necool

"You know, I never thought I'd be this happy," Ellie admitted, her voice soft as she looked into Chloe's eyes. "You make me feel...alive."

Chloe's smile widened, and she pulled Ellie into a tight embrace. "You make me feel the same way, my queen. I'm so glad we found each other. And we were friends first."

Their nights were filled with passion, their bodies entwined in a dance of desire. They would kiss for hours, their lips exploring every inch of each other's skin. Chloe's touch was gentle yet firm, her fingers tracing patterns on Ellie's body that made her gasp with pleasure. Ellie's hands were just as eager, exploring the curves and contours of Chloe's form, eliciting moans that filled the room.

Their lovemaking was wild and unrestrained, the sounds of their passion echoing through the apartment. Zoe, who had been trying to focus on her own dating life, often found herself turning up the TV to drown out the noise. She couldn't help but smile at their happiness, even as she rolled her eyes at the interruptions.

One evening, Ellie and Chloe's passion reached a new level. They explored each other with a fervor that left them both breathless. Chloe's mouth moved from Ellie's lips to her neck, trailing kisses down to her breasts. Ellie arched her back, her fingers tangling in Chloe's hair as she guided her lower. Chloe's tongue danced over Ellie's skin, drawing out a gasp that turned into a moan.

"You taste so good," Chloe whispered, her voice husky with desire. Ellie's response was a soft whimper, her body trembling with anticipation. Chloe's fingers found their way between Ellie's legs, teasing and stroking until Ellie was writhing beneath her.

Their lovemaking was a symphony of sounds and sensations, each touch and kiss building to a crescendo that left them both shuddering with release. As they lay entwined in each other's arms, their breaths slowly returning to normal, Ellie looked into Chloe's eyes and whispered, "I think I love you."

Chloe's smile was radiant, her eyes shining with unshed tears. "I think I love you too, my queen."

Their love was all-consuming, and as the weeks passed, they found themselves wrapped up in each other, almost forgetting about the upcoming Pride party weekend on July 20th. Zoe, who had been planning the event with enthusiasm, often had to remind them of the impending celebration.

Meanwhile, about a week prior, Zoe had decided to expand her dating horizons by joining an international sapphic dating app. We shall see if anything comes of that or what an international dating app is really all about. Apparently, she was feeling open or adventurous.

Ellie and Chloe continued to build their own relationship. When they actually came up for air, they saw more friends. They loved spending Sundays at the dog park with Parker and London, their gay friends who always brought their adorable husky dog Nemo. The dog's Nemo & Max's playful antics often served as a backdrop to their laughter and shared stories.

"You two are so cute together," Parker commented one Sunday, his arm wrapped around London's waist. "It's like you were made for each other."

Ellie smiled, her eyes shining with happiness. "We really are. I can't imagine being with anyone else."

Chloe nodded, her gaze fixed on Ellie. "Neither can I. You're my everything, my queen."

Chapter 7

The Spiritual Experience That Changed Her

———❤———

Rewind, July 9th. The sun dipped below the horizon, casting an ethereal glow over the desert landscape. Zoe sat cross- legged on a yoga mat, her eyes closed, the sound of singing bowls resonating around her. She had been invited to this spiritual soundbath retreat by her best guy friend, Charlie, for his birthday. Accompanying them were their spiritual goddess, Aria, and Charlie's boyfriend, Leo. The desert, with its vast expanse and serene beauty, was the perfect backdrop for a journey of self-discovery and healing.

As the sound waves swooshed over her, Zoe felt a profound sense of peace. The vibrations seemed to echo through her body, releasing tension and opening her heart. She took a deep breath, allowing the energy to flow through her, and in that moment, she felt a presence. It was warm and comforting, a familiar embrace that wrapped around her like a gentle hug. She knew instantly that it was her dad.

Tears streamed down her face as she felt his love, his pride, and his encouragement. It was as if he were standing right beside her, whispering words of comfort and strength. She had never felt so connected to him, so at peace with his passing. It was a healing moment, a gift from the universe that she hadn't expected.

As the soundbath continued, Zoe felt a shift within her. It started as a soft flutter in her chest, growing into a wave of emotion that swept through her entire being. Her guard, which she had held up for so long, began to crumble. She felt vulnerable, raw, and open in a way she hadn't experienced in years. It was both terrifying and exhilarating, a sense of profound openness that left her feeling exposed yet liberated. Almost a feeling as if her chastity heart was now unlocked.

When the soundbath ended, Zoe opened her eyes, her vision blurred by tears. She looked around at the faces of her friends, each of them glowing with a sense of inner peace. Charlie, who had been sitting beside her, reached out and squeezed her hand. "That was intense," he whispered, his voice thick with emotion.

Zoe nodded, unable to find the words to express what she had just experienced. She felt a deep sense of gratitude for this moment, for the healing and the awakening that had taken place within her.

The next day, as they packed up their things and prepared to head back to the city, Zoe felt a sense of lightness. The desert had given her a gift, a sense of renewal and hope that she hadn't known she needed. As they drove, the sun casting a warm glow over the landscape, Zoe's phone buzzed in her pocket. She pulled it out, her eyes scanning the notification. It was a message from the international sapphic dating app she had joined recently.

"Hi, Zoe! Love your name, btw 😊 I'm Sofia, I loved your profile 💕" the message read. "You seem like an incredible person. Would you like to chat?"

Zoe's heart fluttered as she read the message from a woman named Sofia. She looked out the window, a smile spreading across her face. It felt like a sign, a gift from the universe, a confirmation that she was ready to open her heart again.

As the city skyline came into view, Zoe typed a response, her fingers trembling with anticipation. "Hi Sofia, love your profile too! I'd love to chat."

She pressed send. Zoe, not realizing at first the time difference between them and her slight delay in response, she sent the message super late for Sofia. Which later becomes a big factor in their communication. Still, her heart filled with a sense of excitement and possibility. The desert had healed her, the soundbath had awakened her, and now, the universe was sending her a gift. She couldn't wait to see where this new connection would lead.

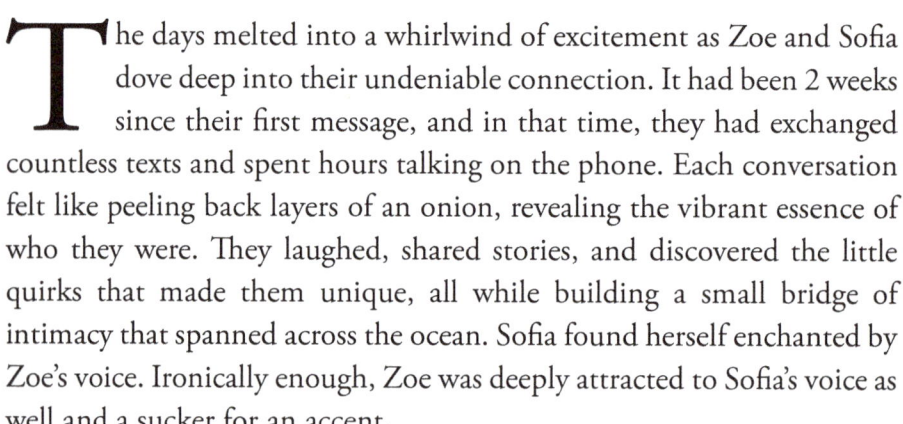

Chapter 8

A Connection Across Continents

The days melted into a whirlwind of excitement as Zoe and Sofia dove deep into their undeniable connection. It had been 2 weeks since their first message, and in that time, they had exchanged countless texts and spent hours talking on the phone. Each conversation felt like peeling back layers of an onion, revealing the vibrant essence of who they were. They laughed, shared stories, and discovered the little quirks that made them unique, all while building a small bridge of intimacy that spanned across the ocean. Sofia found herself enchanted by Zoe's voice. Ironically enough, Zoe was deeply attracted to Sofia's voice as well and a sucker for an accent.

Every word she heard was like a melodic blend of warmth and humor that made her heart race.

Sofia lived in Spain with her cousin, who owned a quaint coffee shop tucked away north of the outskirts of the city's neighborhood. "It's called

Cafe Hecho de Corazón," Sofia shared one evening, her sexy Argentinian accent wrapping around the words like a soft embrace. "I love being a barista; it's like being part of a community, you know?" Zoe's eyes lit up and her tone of voice changed at the mention of coffee.

"That sounds amazing! I used to own a coffee shop here in the States. It was my little haven. I was so passionate about it. I loved creating unique blends for my menu and watching customers' reactions at first sip. I hope to one day own a cafe again." Her voice softened as she reminisced. "There's something magical about coffee. It brings people together, creates connections." Sofia chuckled, a sound that sent a thrill through Zoe. "Maybe we were destined to meet! Two coffee lovers across the world, brewing our dreams one cup at a time."

As they continued to exchange stories, Zoe learned more about Sofia's life in Spain. Sofia described her days filled with laughter with her friends, the smell of fresh coffee, and the vibrant energy of the city she is still getting to know. "I ride my scooter everywhere," she said, her voice bubbling with excitement. "The freedom of the wind in my hair, the sun hits me, and just riding along the streets and I can park anywhere-it's exhilarating." Zoe could almost picture it: Sofia zipping through the streets, her long hair flowing behind her like a kite.

"I've always wanted to visit Spain, especially Barcelona, I've never been," Zoe admitted. "The culture, the food, the art—everything about it seems so alive.""Then you must come! I'll take you to all the best spots," Sofia replied a hint of mischief in her tone. "We'll have coffee and explore the city together. I'll show you the hidden gems that tourists never find. Plus, you'll get to ride on my scooter with me. Is that okay?"

The thought sent a shiver of longing through Zoe. She could almost feel the warmth of her arms around Sofia's waist riding on the back of the scooter, the thrill of experiencing new adventures together. She replied, " Come on, girl, this sounds like a dream, of course, it's okay. I can't wait. Maybe I should really consider coming then; it has been on my list of Europe destinations, and you are there!" But as the days turned into nights, Zoe couldn't shake the feeling that their connection was too good to be true.

Then came the news that turned their conversations into a whirlwind of anticipation.

Chapter 9

GAY PRIDE WEEKEND
PART 1

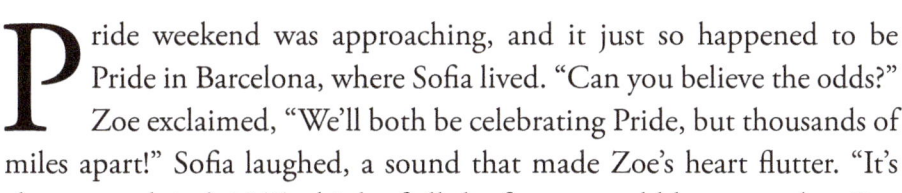

P ride weekend was approaching, and it just so happened to be Pride in Barcelona, where Sofia lived. "Can you believe the odds?" Zoe exclaimed, "We'll both be celebrating Pride, but thousands of miles apart!" Sofia laughed, a sound that made Zoe's heart flutter. "It's almost cruel, isn't it? To think of all the fun we could have together. But maybe it's a sign that we're meant to enjoy our freedom first."

"Yeah, let's enjoy our freedom, babe," Zoe replied, trying to keep her voice light, but the playful banter concealed an underlying yearning. They both understood the weight of the unspoken words hanging between them.

As the weekend approached, they made a pact: to NOT TALK during Pride weekend, allowing themselves to fully immerse in the celebrations with their friends. It was a bittersweet agreement, one that felt necessary yet painful.

"I'll be thinking of you, you know," Sofia teased, her voice laced with a hint of vulnerability. "But I promise to focus on my friends and the festivities."

"Me too," Zoe replied, her heart heavy with the thought of not hearing Sofia's voice. "But we'll have so much to share when we reconnect."

Zoe prepared for the festivities in her city, gathering outfits, planning her outfits, and readying herself for the vibrant celebration of love and identity. She felt a mix of joy and longing, the thrill of the event clashing with the ache of missing someone she had never met in person.

On the day of Pride, Zoe joined her friends—Ellie and Chloe, Charlie, Leo, Parker, London, and Annabella—at the parade. The streets were alive with color, laughter, and love, a kaleidoscope of identities celebrating their truth. Zoe felt the energy wash over her, the warmth of community wrapping around her like a comforting embrace. "Look at all the beautiful people!" Annabella exclaimed, her eyes wide with excitement. "This is what it's all about— celebrating who we are!" Zoe smiled, her heart swelling with pride. "Absolutely! It's a reminder that we're never alone in our journeys." As the parade kicked off, Zoe danced alongside her friends, their laughter echoing through the streets.

They waved flags, throwing glitter everywhere, and embraced the joyous atmosphere. But in the back of her mind, Zoe couldn't help but wonder what Sofia was doing at that very moment. Was she celebrating with friends, dancing in the streets of Barcelona, feeling the same thrill of freedom and love? The day passed in a blur of colors, music, and laughter, but as night fell, Zoe found herself sitting on a bench, her heart weirdly heavy. She pulled out her phone, glancing at the screen. No messages from Sofia.

"Hey, you okay?" Charlie asked, plopping down beside her. "You seem a bit distracted." Zoe sighed, looking out at the crowd. "Just thinking about someone special. It's Pride weekend, and I can't help but wish she were here."

"Is this the girl from the sapphic app?" Charlie asked, a knowing smile on his face.

"Yeah," Zoe admitted, her cheeks flushing. "We've been talking every day. It feels like we have this incredible connection, but we're on opposite sides of the world."

"Love knows no distance," Charlie said, nudging her playfully. "You never know what might happen. Just enjoy the moment." Zoe nodded, taking a deep breath. She tried to focus on the celebration, to let the joy of Pride fill her heart. But as the night wore on, she couldn't shake the feeling of longing.

Meanwhile, across the ocean, Sofia was immersed in her own celebration. The streets of Barcelona were alive with music, laughter, and love. She danced with her friends, the vibrant atmosphere igniting her spirit. But even amidst the festivities, her thoughts drifted to Zoe. "Are you okay?" her cousin asked, noticing Sofia's distracted demeanor. "You seem a bit lost in thought." Sofia smiled, trying to shake off the feeling.

"Just thinking about a friend back in the States. We've been talking a lot lately."

"Friend? Or something more?" her cousin teased, nudging her playfully. Sofia laughed, her heart fluttering at the thought. "Maybe something more. But we made a pact not to talk this weekend. I want to enjoy the moment." As the night unfolded, Sofia danced under the stars, her heart filled with hope and desire. She couldn't help but wonder what Zoe was doing at that very moment if she was feeling the same pull, the same connection that had ignited between them.

Finally, Sofia decided to give in and texted a video of her and the parade and said in the video, "okay, clearly I am failing and breaking our deal. Hi, I'm thinking about you." Zoe's heart and she can't stop smiling, she starts blowing up Sofia's phone for a good ten minutes with photos and videos. She texts, " I've been dying to talk to you. Is it weird I missed you?"

Sofia replies, "love the pics, you look so cute, no it's not weird. I missed you too." Zoe asked if she was having fun and assured her she's been on her mind, and as much as they joked about pride weekend is like being in Vegas, "whatever happens at pride, stays at pride," realistically, they weren't able to stop thinking about one another. They were 9 hours apart on time so when Sofia was finished partying and out late coming back from the pride festivities, Zoe was basically just starting her adventures! Zoe texts again. "okay beautiful, let's try again lol enjoy your friends; i'll be waiting for you to tell me about your weekend and exchange stories," Sofia replies, "okay, besos, talk to you tomorrow." Zoe replies, "i'll be thinking of you."

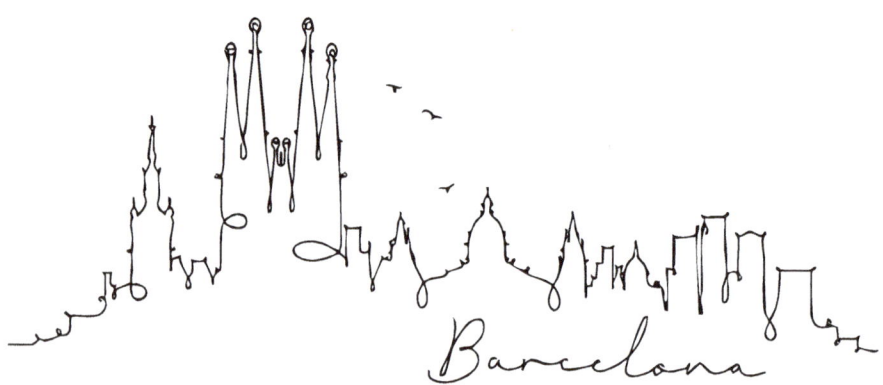

Chapter 10

Pride Part 2 - A Whirlwind of Emotions

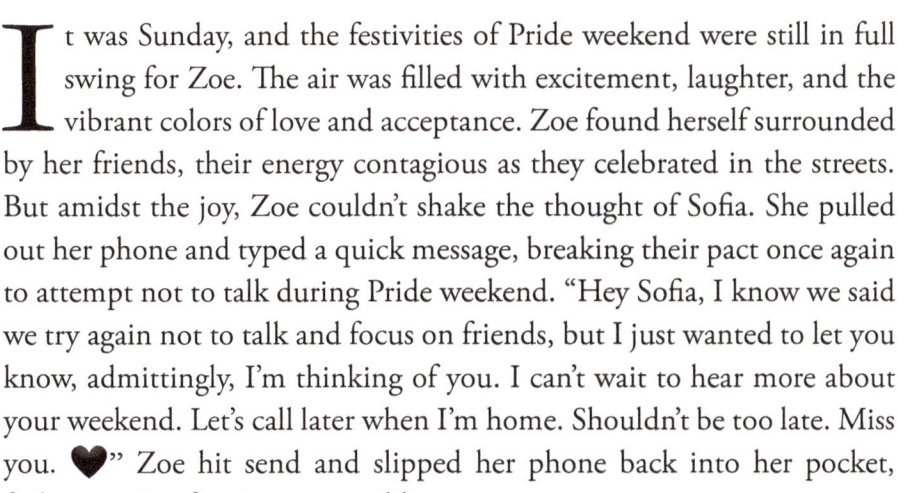

I t was Sunday, and the festivities of Pride weekend were still in full swing for Zoe. The air was filled with excitement, laughter, and the vibrant colors of love and acceptance. Zoe found herself surrounded by her friends, their energy contagious as they celebrated in the streets. But amidst the joy, Zoe couldn't shake the thought of Sofia. She pulled out her phone and typed a quick message, breaking their pact once again to attempt not to talk during Pride weekend. "Hey Sofia, I know we said we try again not to talk and focus on friends, but I just wanted to let you know, admittingly, I'm thinking of you. I can't wait to hear more about your weekend. Let's call later when I'm home. Shouldn't be too late. Miss you. ♥" Zoe hit send and slipped her phone back into her pocket, feeling a mix of excitement and hope.

She pushed the thought aside and threw herself into the celebration, dancing with her friends and soaking up the vibrant atmosphere. As the day turned into night, Zoe found herself caught up in the whirlwind of Pride. She danced with friends, laughed, and drank, the hours slipping by. Before she knew it, it was 1 AM, and she was still going strong, the music pulsing through her veins. She didn't realize how quickly the time had passed, nor did she think about the time difference between her and Sofia.

Meanwhile, across the ocean, Sofia waited. She had checked her phone several times throughout the night, hoping to hear from Zoe. When she finally saw Zoe's message, her heart fluttered with excitement, but as the hours ticked by and she didn't hear back, her excitement turned into disappointment. She tried to shake off the feeling, focusing on her friends and the celebration, but she couldn't help feeling a pang of sadness. The night ended a lot earlier for Sofia, and went to bed without hearing from Zoe. Monday came, and Sofia woke up to still find no new messages from Zoe. She tried to push aside the disappointment, reminding herself that Zoe was probably just caught up in the festivities. But as the day wore on, she couldn't shake the feeling of unease. She checked her phone constantly, hoping to see a notification from Zoe, but there was nothing. Zoe, on the other hand, had partied hard the night before. She had danced until 3 AM, the music and laughter filling her with a sense of euphoria. She had even ended up at an after-party on a boat, the city lights reflecting off the water as she celebrated with friends. By the time she rested her head on the pillow, which was barely before the sun came up, Zoe started to feel guilt.

She woke up the next day, her head pounding and her body aching. She realized she hadn't called Sofia. She groaned, pulling out her phone and checking the time.

It was already 7 PM in Spain, and she knew Sofia would be disappointed. She quickly typed out a message, her heart racing. "Hey Sofia, I'm so sorry I didn't call last night. I got caught up in the festivities and lost track of time. I feel terrible, and I hope you're not too mad at me. Can we talk? I miss you. ♥" Zoe hit send and waited, her stomach churning with anxiety. She knew she had messed up, and she hoped Sofia would understand. She paced back and forth, her mind racing with thoughts of what to say, how to make it right.

Sofia saw the message and felt a mix of relief and frustration. She had been waiting all day to hear from Zoe, and now that she finally had, she couldn't help but feel a pang of disappointment. But as she read Zoe's words, she felt her heart soften. She knew Zoe was genuine, and she couldn't stay mad at her. "Hey Zoe, it's okay. I was a little disappointed, but I understand. Let's talk. I miss you too. ♥ " Zoe's heart leaped with joy as she read Sofia's message. She quickly dialed her number, and when Sofia answered, she could hear the smile in her voice.

"Hey, beautiful," Zoe said, her voice soft. "I'm so sorry about last night. I got caught up in the moment and lost track of time. I feel terrible." Sofia chuckled, her voice warm. "It's okay, Zoe. I understand. Pride weekend is a whirlwind, and it's easy to get swept up in it. I'm just glad to hear from you now." Zoe smiled, feeling a sense of relief wash over her. "I'm so glad you're not mad at me. I missed you so much, and I couldn't stop thinking about you. How was your Pride weekend?" Sofia's voice filled with excitement as she recounted her adventures, the vibrant atmosphere of Barcelona, and the joy of celebrating with friends and her cousin. Zoe listened, heart smiling with happiness as she imagined Sofia dancing in the streets, meeting new people, and just looking so cute. As they talked, the tension between them melted away, replaced by laughter and shared stories.

Zoe apologized again, promising to be more mindful in the future, and Sofia accepted her apology with grace. They talked for hours, their connection deepening with each passing moment. As the night wore on, Zoe and Sofia found themselves lost in conversation, their hearts intertwined. They laughed, shared secrets, and made plans for Zoe to come visit.

Despite the distance between them, they now felt their connection was real, and they were determined to explore it further. "I can't wait to see you, Sofia," Zoe said, her voice soft. "I know it's going to be amazing." Sofia smiled, her heart fluttering with anticipation. "I can't wait either, Zoe. I know it's going to be amazing. We will have fun together." With that, they said their goodbyes, their hearts filled with hope and desire.

As Zoe hung up the phone, she felt a sense of peace wash over her. She knew she had made a mistake, but she also knew that their connection was strong enough to withstand it. She looked forward to the future, to the adventures that lay ahead, and to the possibilities of a love that awaited her.

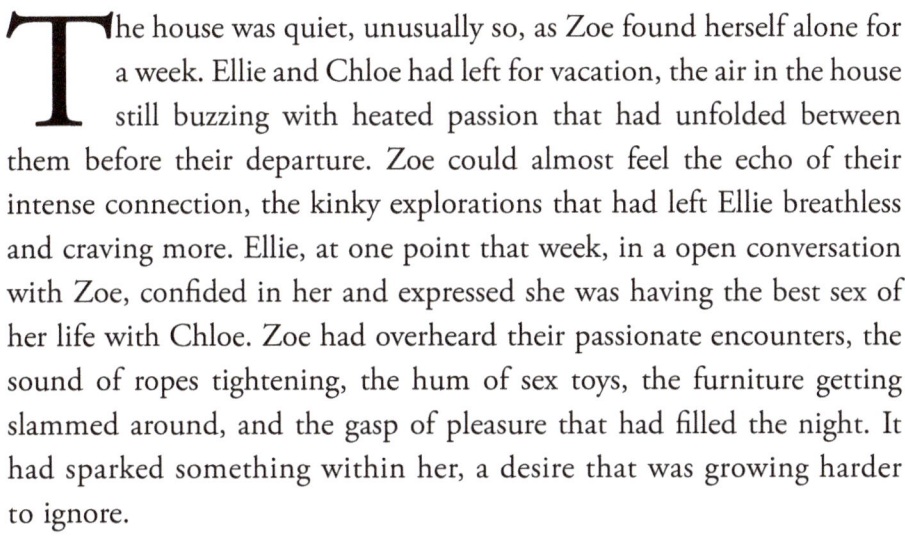

Chapter 11

House of Sex & Desire

The house was quiet, unusually so, as Zoe found herself alone for a week. Ellie and Chloe had left for vacation, the air in the house still buzzing with heated passion that had unfolded between them before their departure. Zoe could almost feel the echo of their intense connection, the kinky explorations that had left Ellie breathless and craving more. Ellie, at one point that week, in a open conversation with Zoe, confided in her and expressed she was having the best sex of her life with Chloe. Zoe had overheard their passionate encounters, the sound of ropes tightening, the hum of sex toys, the furniture getting slammed around, and the gasp of pleasure that had filled the night. It had sparked something within her, a desire that was growing harder to ignore.

Meanwhile, Zoe's connection with Sofia was intensifying. Their initial magnetic pull had evolved into an intense, all-consuming desire. They had agreed to wait, to let their first encounter unfold naturally when they finally met in person. But with each passing night, the staying reserved with words about their desire was weakening. Zoe found herself staying up later and later, her phone calls with Sofia growing longer and more charged.

One evening, as Zoe lay on her bed, the house eerily silent, her phone rang. Sofia's name flashed on the screen, and Zoe felt a familiar flutter in her stomach. She answered, her voice soft, "Hey, beautiful." Sofia's voice was a whisper, her sexy as fuck Argentinian accent more pronounced. "Hey, Zoe. I can't stop thinking about you. It's getting harder to wait. Quiero que vos." Zoe felt a shiver run down her spine. She knew exactly what it meant. "I know, Sofia. I feel it, too. It's like a good desire but almost a pain inside of me."

There was a pause, a soft, slow intake of a breath, and Sofia's voice laced with desire. "Zoe, I want to try something. Do you trust me.?"

Zoe's heart pounded in her chest. She knew where this was going, and she was ready to dive in. " Yes, I trust you."

Sofia's voice grew more confident, taking the lead. "close your eyes, Zoe. Imagine I'm there with you. What would you do first?"

Zoe let her eyes flutter closed, catching her breath as she let her imagination run wild. "I'd touch your face, run my fingers through your long hair, move your bangs out of your face, kiss you softly, feeling your breath on my lips."

Sofia's voice was a soft moan, guiding Zoe further into their shared fantasy. "and I'd kiss you back, Zoe. My hands would explore your body, tracing every curve. I'd unbutton your blue button-down denim shirt slowly, feeling your skin beneath my fingertips."

Zoe's breath gasped, her body responding to Sofia's words. She could almost feel Sofia's touch, her body aching with desire.

They continued to paint a vivid picture with their words, their breath growing heavier, their voices laced with need.

Sofia took control, her voice commanding yet gentle. "I want you to touch yourself, Zoe. Pretend it's me. Feel my hands on you, my lips exploring your body."

Zoe, of course, complied, her hand trembling as she let it wander. Zoe grows more confident, hoping this is what Sofia wants.

She talks in a seductive voice, " I imagine you on top of me, and your legs start to fall in place perfectly with mine. And I would reach over your back and unlatch your bra and have your perfect gorgeous breasts just a few inches in my face." Sofia exhales in response, "Oh my goodness, that's hot, you wanted them in your face, now, what will you do." Zoe replies, " I would start by putting your nipples in my mouth and licking and sucking while my hands are down your back and down onto your ass. And then release your sexy breasts from my mouth so I can kiss your lips." "I love that, Zoe, keep going baby, please, I'm so turned on." Zoe continues, "my fingers slide inside of you and my other hand on your hips, slowly guiding you to trust over me." "oh Zoe, estoy ahi con vos, me sentis.?" Then a break in silence of just them catching their breath Zoe says "si, sexy, I feel you…uuufff you got me baby girl."

The night wore on, their desire melting together, their connection deepening. They exchanged pictures of themselves for them to stare at while they stayed on the phone a little longer. They explored each other's bodies the best they could through whispered words. Zoe says to Sofia, "I can't wait for you to really climax with me."

Both of them realized that was their first intense intimacy, leaving them both craving more. As they finally hung up, their bodies relieved but their desires far from quenched, Zoe knew she was in deep. She was questioning herself, how could it feel possible to be falling for this girl. Regardless of the questioning, she couldn't wait to see where this uncharted territory of desire would lead her.

For now, she lay in her bed, her body still tingling, her mind racing with thoughts of Sofia. She knew she was playing with fire, but she didn't care. She was ready to burn and deal with it later.

Chapter 12

Forests of Magical Friery Passions

Meanwhile, Ellie and Chloe found themselves deep in the heart of the forest, their rented cabin nestled among the towering trees. The air was crisp and filled with the scent of pine, the rustling leaves providing a soothing soundtrack to their escape. They had brought with them a small bag of magic mushrooms, a gift from Leo, who had insisted it would be the perfect way to enhance their adventure.

After settling into the cozy cabin, they decided to take the plunge. Chloe carefully measured out the doses, and they swallowed the mushrooms with a sense of anticipation. As they waited for the effects to kick in, they built a warm fire in the hearth, the crackling flames casting a comforting glow over the room.

Soon, the world began to shimmer. Colors became brighter, sounds more vivid, and their senses heightened. Ellie turned to Chloe, her eyes wide with wonder. "This is amazing," she whispered, her voice echoing in her own ears.

Chloe smiled, her face aglow in the firelight. "It's like seeing the world through a more beautiful lens."

As the night unfolded, their connection deepened. They found themselves drawn to each other, their bodies responding to the heightened sensations.

Ellie leaned in, her lips finding Chloe's in a soft, tender kiss. Chloe's hands wandered, tracing the curves of Ellie's body, the warmth of the fire adding to their growing desire.

They moved to the fuzzy rug in front of the fireplace, their bodies entwined as they explored each other with gentle, loving touches. Taking off layers of clothing one by one until they are just in their underwear. Ellie's fingers danced over Chloe's skin, eliciting soft moans that echoed through the cabin. She noticed Chloe's tattoos more that night, almost as if they were moving slowly with her touch. Ellie, eyes filled with passion and desire, she kept telling Chloe, "You are a goddess, you know that?."

Chloe's lips trailed kisses down Ellie's neck, her breath hot against her skin. Chloe replies "I love when you call me that, and you are my sexy queen."

They took their time, savoring each touch, each sensation, leaving them more and more breathless. Chloe, on top of Ellie, starts to kiss all down the side of her body till she reaches her hips. Her long lioness hair is falling on top of Ellie's skin slightly tickling her with the added sensation of the kisses. Then Chloe starts to move her mouth slowly from the hip to the middle of Ellie's belly button. From there starts to move closer to her underwear and starts to lick and bite around the underwear till she grabs the top of the lacey blue panties with her teeth and starts to pull them down all the way to her feet.

Ellie is shaking and filled with sexual anticipation. Her hips are moving and she starts to slowly squirm. As Chloe pulls off the panties, she starts to suck on Ellie's toes really slowly. She moves her mouth now back to the middle of her right leg and starts to kiss and softly bite Ellie's leg as she slowly pushes her left leg more and more open for her hands to slide up Ellie's thigh, synchronized perfectly with her mouth and tongue moving closer up her right leg. Until her mouth and left hand both meet right at Ellie's lips of her vulva. Chloe, without hesitation, rolls her tongue right into the inner folds, perfectly finding Ellie's clit while simultaneously sliding her index finger on her left hand slowly into Ellie. Ellie's back is arched, and she gasps with a sexy yelp, "Oh my god, babe, that feels so good."

Chloe takes a breath and says, "You taste so fucking good and feel so good, too, baby." and then immediately continues to go down on Ellie. She released her finger out of her vagina and put both hands on Ellie's inner thighs, and started to suck as she was licking her pussy. Ellie's eyes start rolling back until she closes them. Ellie is thinking she's about to cum any minute, so she starts telling Chloe, "I'm so close. You are so fucking good, almost." Within seconds Ellie cums with Chloe's mouth wrapped around her, and Chloe feels Ellie start closing her legs and pulling her up towards her.

As the night wore on, their desires grew wilder. Ellie suggested they move to the hot tub outside, the bubbling water beckoning them with promises of warmth and pleasure. They stepped into the water, the heat enveloping them like a comforting embrace. Their passion ignited, their bodies moving together in a dance of desire. Once again turned on, they couldn't help themselves.

Chloe's hands tangled in Ellie's hair, pulling her closer, their breaths mingling as they kissed with an appetite that left them both gasping. Ellie's fingers dug into Chloe's skin, leaving marks of passion as they moved together, their bodies slick with water and sweat. They clung to the sides of the hot tub, their moans rising through the night as they surrendered to the wild, rough sex that left them both trembling with release.

But their desires were far from sated. As the moon hung high in the sky, they found themselves drawn to the forest, the call of nature irresistible. They ventured out, their bodies still tingling with the effects of the mushrooms, their hearts racing with anticipation.

Under a towering tree, they rolled around on the soft moss, their bodies entwined in a wild dance of desire. The forest seemed to come alive around them, the rustling dirt and the distant hoots of owls adding to the primal energy that coursed through their veins. They explored each other with a bit of savagery that left them both breathless, their bodies moving in sync with the rhythm of the forest.

Their sex was raw and intense, a symphony of moans and gasps that echoed through the trees. They clung to each other, their bodies slick with sweat, their hearts pounding in unison as they surrendered to the wild, untamed passion that consumed them.

As the night wore on, their desires finally sated. They lay entwined under the tree, their breaths slowly returning to normal. The forest seemed to wrap around them like a comforting embrace, the sounds of nature lulling them into a peaceful state.

In the aftermath of their passionate encounters, Ellie and Chloe found themselves talking about their future. The connection they had forged was undeniable, and they knew they wanted to take the next steps together.

Chloe was lying on Ellie's chest. "I want to move in with you," Chloe said softly, her fingers tracing patterns on Ellie's skin. "I want to wake up next to you every morning, to share our lives completely."

Ellie smiled, her heart swelling with love. "I want that too, Chloe. I can't imagine my life without you in it."

They talked about the logistics, about the possibility of Zoe moving out of the apartment by the end of the year, allowing Chloe to move in with Ellie. Zoe always mentioned to Ellie if they got boo'd up one day, that's the only way they'd leave each other as housemates or if one of them wanted to move out of the city. But Ellie and Chloe also considered another option, a dream that had been growing in their hearts.

"What if we moved to the forest?" Ellie suggested, her eyes shining with excitement. "We could build a cabin, I would design it, of course, live surrounded by nature, and create our own little haven."

Chloe's face lit up at the thought. "That sounds perfect. We could have our own garden, grow our own food, grow our own flowers to sell in town, and live in harmony with the world around us."

As they talked, their dreams began to take shape, a future filled with love, adventure, and the promise of a life lived fully. They knew that whatever path they chose, they would face it together, their hearts intertwined, their love unbreakable.

And so, under the starlit sky, surrounded by the beauty of the forest, Ellie and Chloe made a pact to build a future filled with love, passion, and the magic of their shared dreams.

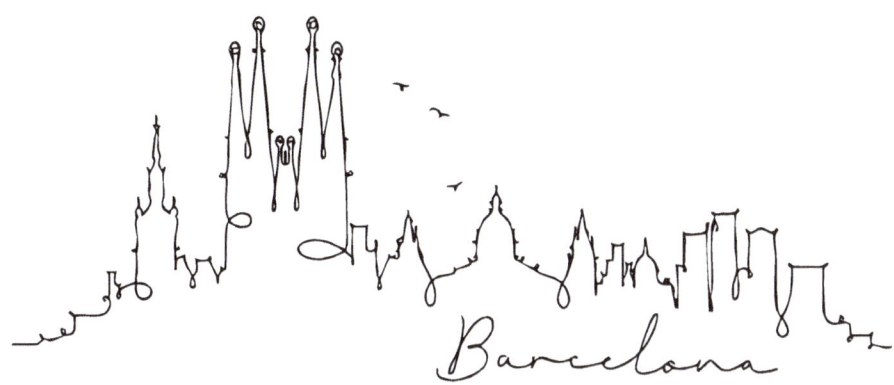

Chapter 13

The Waiting

❤

Zoe sat on her bed, heart racing with excitement and anticipation. This was the 7th time she was on google flights tracking her trip to barcelona and staying up late looking up hotels and configuring the dates for the trip of her dreams. The soft glow of her laptop illuminated the room, casting shadows on the walls as she navigated through the travel website. After weeks of dreaming, talking, and flirting with Sofia, she had finally made the decision to book her trip to Barcelona. She told Sofia the night before that when she woke up, the ticket would be bought. For Zoe, the thought of meeting her crush in person sent butterflies fluttering wildly in her stomach.

With a few clicks, Zoe had secured her flight for the following month. She could hardly believe it. The reality of it all felt surreal. She was going to Spain! The thrill of adventure coursed through her veins, mingling with the sweet anxiety of stepping into the unknown.

She could already picture herself wandering the vibrant streets of Barcelona, exploring the markets, sipping coffee in quaint cafes she had heard about, and, most importantly, wrapping her arms around Sofia for the first time. Zoe loved hugs, and kissing was absolutely her favorite intimate thing to do, so she used to fantasize about their first kiss often.

"Okay, Zoe, you can do this," she whispered to herself, her voice barely above a whisper. "This is your chance to embrace life, to take risks, to be happy."

The weight of her decision settled comfortably on her shoulders. She was still unemployed, but for the first time in a long while, she felt a sense of clarity. She didn't need to have everything figured out right now. What mattered was that she was following her heart, listening to the whispers of her dad in spirit, reminding her to live fully and fearlessly.

As she sat there, lost in her thoughts, her phone buzzed beside her. It was a message from Sofia.

"Hola Bonita! I just saw the cutest little café in downtown Barcelona that I can't wait to take you to! Besides my cousin's cafe, which is a bit further away, they have the best coffee & vibe in town."

Zoe's heart soared at the message. "I can't wait! I just booked my flight! I'll be there in a month!" she replied, her fingers dancing across the screen.

"OMG! This is so exciting! I can't believe we're finally going to meet! It feels like a dream!" Sofia responded almost instantly.

Zoe couldn't help but smile, her cheeks flushing with warmth. "It really does! I've been thinking about you nonstop. I can't wait to explore the city together."

Their conversation flowed effortlessly, filled with playful banter and flirty exchanges. They talked about their favorite foods, the sights Zoe wanted to see, and the little adventures they would embark on together. Zoe felt like a giddy schoolgirl, her heart racing with every message. Sofia tells Zoe, "I will ask my cousin for the week off so I can spend the most time with you in the city and stay at your hotel with you. Is that okay?" Zoe responds with a giggle, "Yes, of course, babe. I was hoping for that."

Later that evening, Zoe decided it was time to share her exciting news with her sister, Mia. They had always been close, and Mia had been a pillar of support throughout Zoe's journey of healing and self-discovery.

"Hey, Mia! You'll never guess what I just did!" Zoe exclaimed as she FaceTimed her sister.

Mia's eyes widened with curiosity. "What? Tell me!"

"I booked a trip to Barcelona to meet Sofia! We've been talking for weeks, and I can't believe I'm actually going!" Zoe's voice bubbled with excitement.

Mia's face lit up with joy. "Oh my Gosh, Zoe! That's amazing! I'm so proud of you! You deserve this happiness!"

Zoe felt a wave of relief wash over her. "Thanks, sis. It feels like a huge step in healing, you know? I know I'm still unemployed and trying to figure things out, but this feels right."

Mia's voice turned serious yet sweet. "You're following your heart, and that's what matters. Don't worry about the job right now. Just focus on this adventure and the joy it brings you. Just like Dad, babe, I believe in you. You're going to love Spain, it's my favorite country, so happy you are going, truly."

Zoe smiled, grateful for her sister's unwavering support. They spent the next hour chatting about the trip, discussing what Zoe should pack, and brainstorming fun activities to do in Barcelona.

As they wrapped up their call, Zoe felt a sense of clarity. She was ready to embrace this new chapter of her life, to explore the untapped territories of desire and adventure.

Meanwhile, in the days that followed, Zoe found herself diving deeper into her connection with Sofia. They continued to text and video chat, their conversations growing more intimate and playful. At one point, they exchanged almost naked photos, experiencing the thrill of vulnerability.

Zoe felt a rush of excitement every time she received a message from Sofia, her heart smiling at the thought of their upcoming meeting.

As the weeks passed, Zoe also confided in her friends about her trip and the possibly blossoming connection with Sofia. She gathered them for a casual get-together at their favorite corner gay dive bar and sat at their usual corner table.

"Okay, spill the tea, Zoe! We want all the details!" Annabella exclaimed, her eyes sparkling with mischief.

Zoe laughed, feeling a sense of warmth wash over her. "I booked a trip to Barcelona to meet Sofia! We've been talking for weeks, and I can't wait to finally see her in person."

Charlie's eyebrows shot up in surprise. "No way! That's incredible! The girl you were missing over Pride weekend? Awe, are you nervous?"

"A little," Zoe admitted, her fingers fidgeting with the big ice cube in her old-fashioned cocktail. "But mostly excited. It feels like a dream come true."

Parker leaned in a playful grin on his face. "You're going to have the time of your life! Just remember to take lots of pictures. We want to see every moment!"

Zoe nodded, her heart swelling with gratitude for her friends' support. "I will! I just hope everything goes smoothly. I want to make the most of this trip." Leo flares his hands and snaps his fingers smirking, and says, "Bitch, I know you're going to fall in love."

As the conversation flowed, laughing, Zoe felt a sense of belonging. She was surrounded by friends who believed in her and encouraged her to chase her dreams and embrace love.

Meanwhile, Ellie had been busy planning her future with Chloe. The idea of moving to the forest, away from the hustle and bustle of city life, had taken root in her mind. She envisioned a cozy cabin surrounded by nature, a place where they could grow their own food, cultivate a garden, and live in harmony with the world around them.

One evening, Ellie brought up the idea with Chloe while they were lounging on the couch, their fingers intertwined. "What if we really did it? What if we found a piece of land in the forest and built our dream home together?"

Chloe's eyes sparkled with excitement. "I love that idea! Just imagine waking up and Maxie staring squirrels out the window and the smell of fresh flowers. It sounds like paradise."

Ellie grinned, feeling a rush of enthusiasm. "We could design it together, create a space that reflects who we are. It would be our little sanctuary."

As they talked about their dreams, Zoe felt a sense of inspiration wash over her. She realized that life was about taking risks, embracing the unknown, and following her heart. She was ready to step into this new chapter, to explore the depths of her connection with Sofia, and to support her friends in their journeys as well.

With each passing day, Zoe felt more confident in her decision to travel to Barcelona. She was ready to embrace whatever adventures awaited her, to dive into love, and to discover the beauty of life in all its forms.

She was ready to chase her dreams, to explore the uncharted territories of desire, and to embrace the magic that lay ahead.

Chapter 14

The Red Bitch Fairy

—♡♥♡—

Zoe sat on her bed, the soft hum of her laptop filling the room. She had been scrolling through her messages with Sofia for what felt like hours, her heart racing with a mix of excitement and anxiety. Their conversations had been filled with flirtation and promises of what was to come when they finally met in person. They had talked about kissing, exploring the city together, and the passionate nights that awaited them. But now, as the date of her trip loomed closer, Zoe couldn't shake the feeling of unease that had settled in her stomach.

It had been almost a week since Sofia suggested they take a step back to create some distance before the trip. "I just feel like I'm putting too much into this virtual relationship," Sofia had said, her voice tinged with uncertainty. "What if it's not what we think it is? I don't want to build up expectations that might not be real."

Zoe had agreed, trying to mask the disappointment that bubbled beneath the surface. They had both felt the connection, the magnetic pull that drew them together, but the fear of the unknown was a heavy weight on their hearts. "Okay, let's take a break. We can reconnect when I arrive," Zoe had replied, forcing the words even though her heart felt heavy.

Now, with only a few days until her departure, Zoe found herself spiraling into a whirlwind of emotions. The excitement of traveling to Barcelona was tinged with anxiety. What if Sofia didn't feel the same way when they finally met? What if the chemistry they had shared through their screens didn't translate in person?

She sighed, running a hand through her hair, her thoughts racing. The reality of the situation hit her hard: she would be on her period during the first three days of her trip. She had dubbed it the "red bitch fairy," a term that made her chuckle despite her anxiety. It felt like a cruel twist of fate, the buildup of anticipation overshadowed by the looming presence of her monthly visitor. Would she be able to enjoy herself? Would she feel sexy?

Zoe pulled out her phone, scrolling through her messages with her friends. She needed to talk to someone to vent her worries and fears. She decided to reach out to Annabella, who always had a knack for lifting her spirits.

"Hey, girl! Can we chat?" Zoe texted, her fingers trembling with anticipation

"Of course! What's up?" Annabella replied almost instantly.

Zoe took a deep breath, her heart racing. "I'm feeling really anxious about my trip to Barcelona. I haven't talked to Sofia in days, and I'm worried about how things will go when I finally meet her. Plus, I'll be on my period, and I'm freaking out about it! I'm pissed, you know? I want to feel good."

Annabella's response came quickly, her energy practically radiating through the screen. "Girl, first of all, you're going to be amazing! And second, the red bitch fairy can't ruin your trip! Just think of it as an opportunity to bond over some wine and chocolate. You'll be fine!"

Zoe couldn't help but smile at Annabella's infectious enthusiasm. "You always know how to cheer me up. But what if Sofia isn't into me when we meet? What if the chemistry is just in my head?"

"Listen, Zoe," Annabella replied, her tone serious yet supportive. "You've built a connection with Sofia that's real. You're both excited to meet, and that means something. Just be yourself, and don't put too much pressure on it. It's going to be an adventure, and you'll figure it out together."

Zoe nodded, feeling a bit of the weight lift off her shoulders. "You're right. I need to just go with the flow and enjoy the experience."

"Exactly! And if you need a little extra boost, just remember to pack your favorite sexy outfit. Confidence is key, even with the red bitch fairy in town!" Annabella added, her playful tone making Zoe laugh.

"Okay, I'll take your advice. Thank you, Annabella. You're the best!" Zoe replied, feeling grateful for her friend's unwavering support.

As the days passed, Zoe's excitement began to overshadow her anxiety. She spent her evenings packing her suitcase, carefully choosing outfits that made her feel confident and beautiful. She selected a cute black dress she'd never worn before but wanted to pack it in case they had a sexy date night. Also, of course, the sexy black-on-black outfit that she knew would make her feel confident and chic.

On the morning of her departure, Zoe woke up with a mix of emotions swirling within her. She felt a surge of excitement, but the anxiety was still there, gnawing at her. She glanced at the calendar and reminded herself that she was embarking on a new adventure, a journey that could lead to something beautiful.

As she made her way to the airport, Zoe couldn't help but replay the moments she had shared with Sofia in her mind. Their late-night conversations, the laughter, the shared dreams of exploring the city together—it all felt so real. She just hoped that when they finally met, the magic would still be there.

The flight was long, and Zoe found herself unable to sleep. Her mind raced with thoughts of Sofia, the anticipation building within her. She imagined their first meeting, the moment their eyes would lock, the excitement of finally being in the same space. What if she didn't live up to Sofia's expectations? What if she was just a figment of her imagination?

As the plane touched down in Barcelona, Zoe felt a rush of adrenaline. She was here, in a new country, ready to embrace whatever came her way. The sun shone brightly, casting a warm glow over the city as she stepped out of the airport, taking a deep breath of the fresh air.

Zoe pulled out her phone, her heart racing as she sent a quick message to Sofia. "I just landed! Can't wait to see you!"

Sofia's response came almost instantly. "Welcome to Spain, baby, I'm so excited! I'll be there in 30 minutes. Get ready for an adventure!"

As she waited, Zoe felt a mix of nerves and anticipation. She glanced at the time, her heart pounding in her chest. She was about to meet the woman who had captured her heart and attention from thousands of miles away, and she couldn't shake the feeling of vulnerability that washed over her.

Zoe is so nervous and meets Sofia at the bottom of the hotel lobby. Sofia is nervous as well and is hoping Zoe is everything she imagined. Sofia wants to show Zoe a good time in the city but was hoping for an immediate romance. Zoe, embarrassed and in severe pain, is struggling to act like her period isn't ruining the parade of this magical experience.

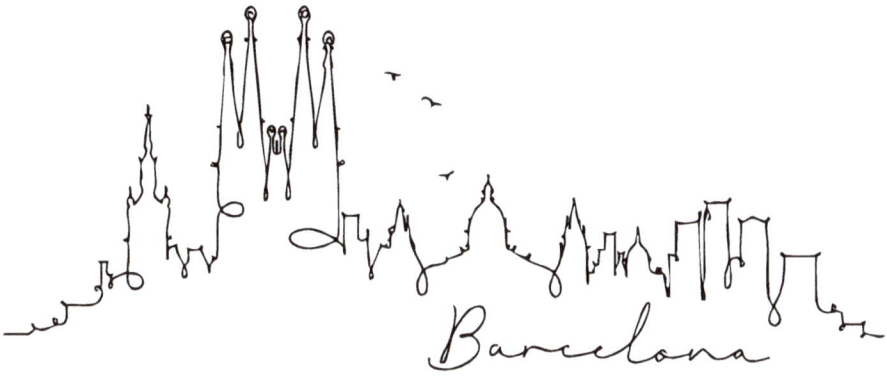

Chapter 15

The Weight of Reality

━━━━◦♥◦━━━━

Zoe sat there at the hotel lobby bar, staring at Sofia but lost in her own world at the same time. She had imagined this moment for so long, yet reality was proving to be a different beast altogether. The sun shone brightly through the window they sat near, casting a golden hue over the city streets, but all Zoe could focus on was the discomfort that radiated from her lower abdomen, a constant reminder of her period's unwelcome presence.

They had just spent the afternoon exploring the Gothic Quarter, and Zoe had tried her best to keep up the façade of excitement, but the pain was becoming increasingly difficult to mask.

"Are you okay?" Sofia's voice broke through her thoughts, concern etched on her face as she glanced at Zoe.

"Yeah, just a little in pain, maybe a little nervous still," Zoe replied, forcing a smile. "It's been a long day of travel and exploring."

Sofia nodded, her expression softening. "Let's get a drink to loosen up the nerves and pain. I know a great place nearby."

As they walked, Zoe felt a mix of gratitude and frustration. She was thrilled to be with Sofia, but the discomfort from her period was a relentless cloud hanging over her. She wanted to be carefree and fun, to enjoy every moment of their time together, but instead, she felt like she was radiating off an insecure vibe.

The bar was quaint, with outdoor seating that overlooked a small plaza filled with locals and tourists alike. Zoe settled into her chair, grateful for the chance to rest. Sofia ordered them both Vermouth, her Argentinian accent adding a sexy quality to her words. Zoe watched her, mesmerized by her effortless charm and beauty, and for a fleeting moment, the pain subsided as she lost herself in Sofia's laughter.

"Salud!" Sofia places the drink in front of Zoe and sits down across from her but leans in closer as they cheer their glasses together. "So, what do you think of Barcelona so far?"

"It's incredible," Zoe replied, taking her first sip of vermouth. The flavor enveloped her senses, momentarily distracting her from the discomfort. "I love the architecture and the energy of the city. It's so alive. Different, it's gorgeous."

Sofia smiled, her eyes sparkling with enthusiasm. "I'm glad you're enjoying it! There's so much more to see. I have a few places in mind for us to visit tomorrow. I'll take us on my scooter."

Zoe's heart raced at the thought of spending more time with Sofia, but a nagging doubt crept in. She wanted to show Sofia how much she cared, to express the romantic feelings that had grown over their virtual conversations, but the pressure of her red bitch fairy coming on this vacation uninvited and the exhaustion from travel made her feel less than her best.

As the afternoon sun began to dip lower in the sky, casting long shadows across the city, Zoe felt a surge of determination. She wanted to kiss Sofia, to break the invisible barrier between them and solidify the connection they had built. What if she was too self-conscious? What if she couldn't perform the way she hoped? After many nights of building up the anticipation and sex talks, she feared waiting any longer would make Sofia feel like the attraction and romance were not there.

"Zoe, are you alright?" Sofia's voice pulled her back to the moment, her brow furrowed with concern.

"Yeah, just thinking," Zoe said, forcing another smile. "I'm really glad to be here with you, smiling at you in person." Zoe's eyes started to sparkle.

"Me too," Sofia replied softly, her gaze lingering on Zoe's face. "I've been looking forward to this for so long. I can't believe you're here."

The sincerity in Sofia's voice sent a thrill through Zoe, and she felt a rush of courage. Maybe this was the moment. Maybe they could bridge the gap of uncertainty that had loomed over their relationship since the start.

"Can I ask you something?" Zoe ventured, her heart racing.

"Claro, of course," Sofia replied, leaning in slightly, her interest piqued.

Zoe took a deep breath, her mind racing with possibilities. "Do you think we could... I mean, would you be okay... if I kissed you?"

Sofia's eyes widened slightly, and for a moment, Zoe feared she had crossed a line. But then Sofia's lips curled into a warm smile. "I'd love that, yes."

Zoe's heart soared as she leaned in, their faces inches apart. The world around them faded, and all she could focus on was Sofia's soft gaze and the warmth radiating from her. As their lips met, a spark ignited between them, a gentle connection that sent shivers down Zoe's spine.

But as quickly as the magic began, Zoe felt a wave of discomfort wash over her. The pain in her abdomen surged, and she pulled back, a mix of embarrassment and frustration flooding her senses. "I'm sorry," she stammered, her cheeks flushed. "It's just—"

"Hey, it's okay," Sofia reassured her, her voice gentle. "You don't have to apologize."

Zoe felt a knot tighten in her chest with slight anxiety. She wanted to be the confident, sexy woman she had imagined, but instead, she felt vulnerable and exposed. "I just… I want to be more present, but my body is not cooperating."

Sofia reached across the table, her hand warm and comforting as it enveloped Zoe's. "I get it. We can take things slow. We have the whole week ahead of us."

Zoe nodded, appreciating Sofia's understanding. But as the day wore on, the reality of her situation began to weigh heavily on her. They spent the rest of the afternoon wandering the streets, but Zoe felt increasingly self-conscious overshadowing her excitement.

As night fell, they found themselves at a small restaurant, the ambiance cozy and inviting. Zoe tried to enjoy the delicious food and Sofia's company, but as the conversation flowed, she felt the pressure building. She wanted to be the fun, carefree version of herself, but with every laugh, every smile, the discomfort nagged at her. The pressure of reclaiming herself and the moment was like a cloud over her.

By the end of the night, Zoe felt drained. They walked back to the hotel, and Zoe's heart raced with a mix of anticipation and anxiety. She wanted to kiss Sofia again, to feel that connection, but the weight of her period embarrassment loomed large.

As they reached the door, Zoe turned to Sofia, her heart pounding. "Can we talk?"

Sofia nodded, her expression serious. "Of course."

Zoe took a deep breath, her emotions swirling. "I really like you, Sofia. I want this to be special, but I'm struggling with… everything."

Sofia's expression softened, and she stepped closer. "I like you too, Zoe. But I also feel like there's a lot of pressure right now. I don't want to force anything."

Zoe felt a shift in the air. "What do you mean? I don't think we are forcing anything.?"

"I just… I'm not sure I'm feeling the romantic spark like I thought I would," Sofia admitted, her voice gentle yet firm. "I want to enjoy our time together without the pressure of expectations."

Zoe's heart sank, a wave of disappointment crashing over her. "So, what does that mean exactly?"

Sofia sits on the bed and tells Zoe to sit down next to her.

Sofia sighed, running a hand through her hair. "I think we should just hang out and see where the week takes us. No pressure for anything romantic. Is that okay?"

Zoe felt a wall go up inside her, a protective barrier against the hurt. "I understand," she replied, forcing a smile that didn't quite reach her eyes. "I just thought… I thought we had something special built up and still left to explore. I also thought you would give it more time to feel it out. But okay, I get it, ya, let's just hang out like friends."

Sofia sits closer, her eyes searching Zoe's face. "We do have something special, Zoe. I just don't want to rush into anything. Let's enjoy each other's company and see where it leads. Even if it's just this week."

Zoe nodded, but inside, she tried not to feel a profound sense of loss.

She wanted to be open and vulnerable, to embrace the connection they had built, but now she felt like she had to guard her heart.

Zoe instantly felt sad and put her guard up completely, and didn't want to feel open and vulnerable anymore.

As they got ready for bed, unsure if she should cuddle her, Zoe couldn't shake the feeling that Sofia had judged her too soon, not allowing her to show "the real Zoe"—the one who was fun, passionate, and ready for adventure. Zoe felt so embarrassed and speechless.

As she laid in bed that night, the city's sounds fading into the background, Zoe felt the weight of reality settles over her like a heavy blanket. She had come to Barcelona seeking connection and romance, but now she was left feeling more alone than ever, her heart guarded against the very person she thought would bring it more to life.

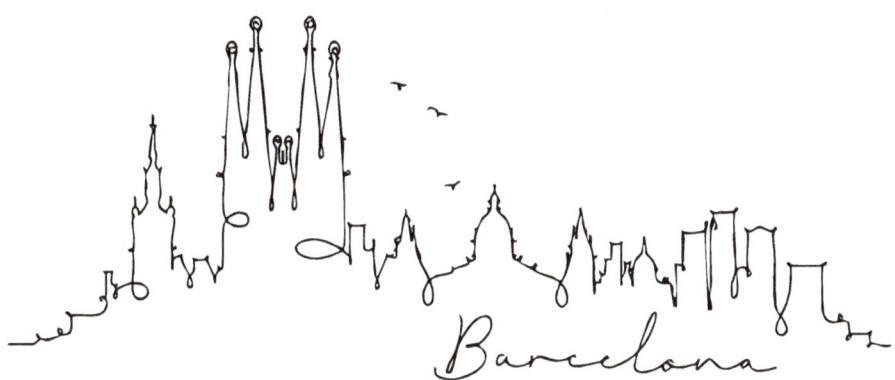

Chapter 16

Unfolding of Unexpecting Intimacies

━━━━━❤━━━━━

Z oe and Sofia had reached day three of their Barcelona trip, and the weight of Zoe's initial disappointment still lingered. Her guard was up a protective barrier that she couldn't quite shake off.

However, as the days passed, Sofia found herself relaxing more, enjoying Zoe's company without the pressure of romantic expectations. The vibe between them slowly started to change, becoming lighter and more playful.

On their third day, they found themselves wandering the streets of Barcelona, their laughter echoing through the bustling city. They visited the Sagrada Familia, marveling at its architectural beauty, and stopped by a local market to sample fresh fruit and a bottle of Vermouth for later. As they walked, they started to make fun of each other, their laughter filling the air and easing the tension that had been present since Zoe's arrival.

"You know, I've been trying to learn some Spanish," Zoe admitted as she was climbing onto the back of Sofia's scooter. "But I'm not very good at it. Still Practicing." as she puts on her helmet.

Sofia smiled, her eyes sparkling with amusement. "Oh, really? Why don't you try saying something in Spanish?" as she's putting on her helmet after asking her that.

Zoe hesitated for a moment before taking a deep breath. "Okay, wait, como se dice: Sit, the word sit."

Sofia responds before pulling the plastic shield down on her helmet. "Siéntate"

Zoe grabs onto Sofia, and as they start to ride the streets, Zoe says as close as she can, hoping Sofia can hear her through the helmets and street noise. "Tu cara es bonita. Ven y siéntate en mi cara."

Sofia burst into laughter, her cheeks flushing with surprise. Turns her head halfway back towards Zoe. "Did you just ask me to sit on your face?"

Zoe smirking. "Maybe. Por que, Is that not how you say it?"

Sofia laughed even harder, shaking her head. "Oh, Zoe. You're something else. Is that what you wanted to learn how to say? Curious, when will you use that."

Their laughter continued, the tension between them slowly dissipating. Later that day, as they rode Sofia's scooter through the city, Zoe continued to hold onto Sofia tightly, her arms wrapped around her waist. The wind whipped through their hair, and Zoe felt a sense of freedom that she hadn't experienced since her arrival.

As day five approached, the dynamic between Zoe and Sofia shifted even more. They found themselves drawn to each other, their connection deepening with each passing moment.

They spent the day exploring the city, their laughter, and playful banter creating a sense of intimacy that was hard to ignore.

That evening, as they returned to the hotel, they couldn't deny the spark that had been ignited between them. They looked at each other, their eyes filled with a mixture of desire and uncertainty. Without a word, they both knew what was about to happen.

As they entered the hotel room, the air was charged with anticipation. Zoe's period had finally ended, and she felt a sense of relief wash and confidence over her. She was ready to explore the connection she had been longing for since her arrival.

They didn't waste any time. Their clothes hit the floor, and they found themselves entwined on the bed, their bodies moving in sync. Their kisses were passionate, and sometimes, their hands exploring every inch of each other's skin.

Zoe, taking control and fluttering with excitement, finally getting to taste Sofia. She found her way down to her vagina lips. As Zoe starts to lick slowly on one side of Sofia's outer lips, she softly slides her tongue through the inner lips and starts to hear Sofia moan in pleasure. Zoe bends her body back with her ass in the air and gets comfy with her face down into Sofia as she spreads her legs open with her hands. The motion of Zoe's tongue and mouth has Sofia rolling her eyes, biting her own lip, and reaching her hands from her face to Zoe's hair, caressing it as she tells her how good it feels.

Zoe starts to wrap Sofia's legs around her back, and as she slowly slides down so that she's laying down and Sofia's legs wrapped around her mid back, she starts rolling her tongue and pressing her lips harder but sensually and at the same time. She finds a rhythm Sofia likes, and as she's about to orgasm, she sucks on her clit in a perfect gasping timeframe for Sofia to climax. Right in her mouth, Zoe feels it all.

It's safe to say their first encounter was intense, and Zoe did not disappoint. Sofia was blown away by the chemistry between them, her body responding to Zoe's touch in ways she hadn't expected.

"Oh goodness, Zoe," Sofia gasped, her body trembling with aftershocks. "That was... incredible. Mmmm fuck, the best."

Zoe smiled, her heart swelling with happiness for Sofia and for herself. "I'm so glad you enjoyed it."

Their intimacy didn't stop there. They basically spent the next two days locked in the hotel room, their passion for each other growing with each encounter. They had shower sex, the water cascading over their bodies as they moved together.

They made love by the window, the city lights casting a warm glow over their naked forms. The sofa had their scent and sex sweat all over it as every time they tried to get ready to go out somewhere, they would attack one another.

They even ordered a sex toy as they wondered what it would be like to try everything since the chemistry was there, but they weren't sure if ever see each other again after this. They felt they might as well have no barriers or rules when sleeping together.

As the random-sized dildo and cheap strap-on arrived, which was hilarious itself to have to blindly order it online. They grabbed it from the delivery guy. They were so nervous and excited. Sofia, with desire and passion in her eyes, asked Zoe, "Have you ever done this before, fucking a girl with a strap-on?."

Zoe replied, " Yes, I have. Usually, I am the one wearing it & only if the girl really wants me to."

"Sounds hot, fuck, well, I want you to. Will you please fuck me tonight?." Sofia replies as she starts to kiss Zoe.

Zoe tries to figure out this ridiculous contraption they had to get as their only choice and make it work and slips into sexy mode quickly. Zoe looks at Sofia and takes her time kissing her, and as she's on top of Sofia, she says, "You're so fucking beautiful." As they lock eyes, Zoe slides herself and the small strap-on toy into Sofia and holds her tighter. Zoe is kissing her neck and listening to Sofia with every move, trying to find the positions and rhythm she enjoys most. Building up how hot the situation is, Sofia leans into Zoe more and more and pushes her body more onto hers. Sofia loves the weight of Zoe on top of her. Sofia tells Zoe, "I love the way you're fucking me right now. I'm there, baby. You almost got me". This being their 4th orgasm together. Sofia quickly flips around and kisses Zoe, thanking her for that experience. Sofia pulls the strap-on off of Zoe. She looks at her, moving hair out of her face, and asks her, "And have you ever done this before, like let someone else do this to you." Zoe replies softly, "No, not really, well, okay, maybe, on rare occasions. I have to really connect with someone." Sofia asks " Can I? Want me to? I want to." Zoe, with no hesitation and filled with trust, kisses her and says "Yes." Zoe is so turned on by Sofia's desire to fuck her and also her sexy feminine yet fit body on top of her perfectly. Her sexy arms holding herself up above Zoe, she experiences so much more pleasure than expected! While watching her triceps flex, her big delicious tits hovering above her, and her perfect abs tighten as she's on top of her, Zoe surprisingly climaxes quickly as well.

They fucked and made love, their connection deepening with each intimate moment. They finally order room service since their appetites were fueled by their passionate encounters. The room attendant who delivered their meal must have sensed their passionate evening and had them rolling in laughter as he asked the ladies if they needed anything else to call him personally. And he had a key, so they didn't have to get up to let him in with whatever they ordered. They soon felt uncomfortable after that comment and asked him to leave, and they were okay. They were all set for service the rest of the night. Still, they laughed so much from that scenario. "Did he really just say, "I have a key, you don't have to get up""

"What the heck was that," Zoe and Sofia repeated the conversation and filled the room with laughter. "Full service here apparently is normal," Sofia laughs.

As they lay entwined in bed, their bodies slick with sweat and their hearts racing, they knew that they had found something special.

The weight of reality had lifted temporarily, replaced by a sense of connection and intimacy that they had both been longing for.

"I'm so glad I came to Barcelona," Zoe whispered, her voice soft as she looked into Sofia's eyes. "I never expected this, but I'm so grateful for it."

Sofia smiled, her heart filled with warmth. "Me too, Zoe. Me too."

And so their connection deepened, and the race for time was almost forgotten. This trip and experience were almost over. Will they continue this connection?

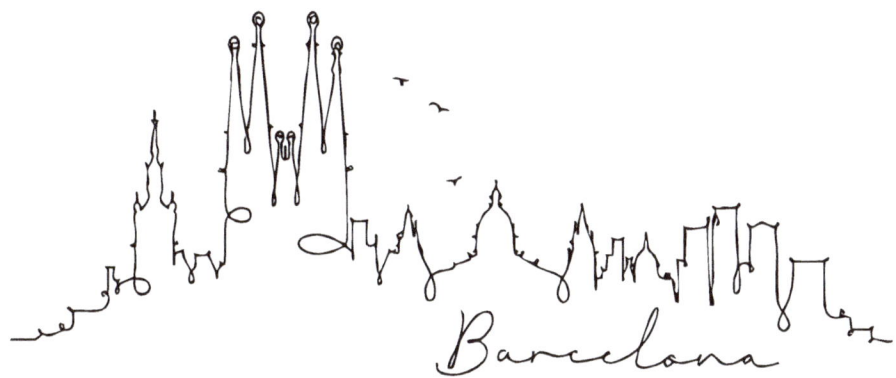

Chapter 17

She likes her, he likes her not.

———♡♥♡———

Z oe and Sofia woke up to the soft glow of the sun slightly painting the room through the hotel curtains. They had spent the entire day in bed, their limbs entwined, their hearts beating in sync. As the day wore on, they both felt a shift, a sense of attachment that was becoming harder to ignore. They had let their guards down, and now, they were in deep.

"Let's have dinner on the rooftop tonight," Zoe suggested, her voice soft as she traced patterns on Sofia's bareback. "It's our last night together, after all."

Sofia felt a pang in her heart at the reminder, but she smiled nonetheless. "I'd love that."

The rooftop was bathed in the warm glow of string lights, the city sprawling out beneath them like a sparkling canvas. Just an incredible view. They felt all for just them. They talked and laughed over elegant fish dishes and a bottle of wine, their hands brushing against each other, their eyes locked in a dance of unspoken words. As the night wore on, their conversation turned into stolen kisses, each one filled with a sense of urgency and longing.

They made their way back to the hotel room, their lips never parting. Sofia couldn't keep her hands off Zoe and told her she wanted to go slow tonight and indulge in her. Sofia lays Zoe down, leaving her sexy black lingerie on while she slowly kisses her body. She pulls only a portion of the top down to grab her boobs and kiss them but then moves down to her waist and starts to unlatch the part on the bottom that snaps in the bodysuit-type lingerie down there and exposes her lips. Zoe is gasping in passion, hard to lay still, and wants to touch Sofia. However, she obeys Sofia on her request. "Zoe, let me have you, please," Sofia says. Sofia starts to play with Zoe, slowly licking her outer and inner lips. She starts to touch her with her fingers and slowly rubbing on her clit and slides down into her vagina, so perfectly synced with her thumb hitting her clit. After a few moans from Zoe, Sofia wanted to smother her mouth on her juicy clit. She removed her fingers and went for it. Her mouth on Zoe made her perfectly explode. Aftershocks of her orgasm swirled in her as Sofia held her for a few minutes without talking. They obviously have and share a fiery connection. One in these moments they can't deny.

As they lay entwined in the aftermath, they couldn't ignore the elephant in the room any longer. Zoe's flight back home was in a few hours, and the reality of their situation was starting to sink in.

Zoe broke the silence first, her voice barely a whisper. "I don't know what to say, Sofia. I never expected this. I feel like I was so open to anything. Now that I met you… I'm going to miss you."

Sofia sighed, her eyes glistening with unshed tears. "Me neither, Zoe. Me neither. I'm going to miss you too."

They fell asleep holding each other, their hearts heavy with the weight of their unspoken feelings. When morning came, Zoe felt a sense of dread wash over her. She didn't know what to say, didn't know how to express the turmoil of emotions inside her.

As she packed her bags, Sofia sat on the bed, her eyes filled with tears. "Zoe," she started, her voice choking with emotion. "I... I can't do this. I can't do long distance. I know we both said that before, that we couldn't. And I can't have a committed relationship right now anyway. I will end up resenting myself or you if I rush into something. I know it's my fault for joining a dating app if I wasn't ready, but I don't regret meeting you. I'm just not able to offer more."

Zoe felt her heart start to shatter into a million pieces. She sat down next to Sofia, taking her hand. "Sofia, I understand. I do. But I can't help but feel something real with you. I don't know what to do from this point. However, I hear you and completely understand."

Sofia cried, her tears streaming down her face. "I feel it too, Zoe. I'm sorry. I can be friends, I still want you in my life, but I can't do anything more than that right now. Is that okay with you, or do you not want to talk to me anymore? I'll understand."

Zoe felt a lump form in her throat, but she nodded, understanding Sofia's decision. Zoe replied to Sofia in a soft, low voice and grabbed her hand.

"Can you give me a couple days to process everything you're saying and what this means and get back to you.?"

Sofia shakes her head and says, "Of course, yes, this is sad, I know, but let me know, and I'd like to keep you in my life somehow, if possible." Zoe is silent and distraught on the way to the airport. As she boarded her flight home, she felt a mix of emotions swirling inside her. She was sad, overwhelmed, and distressed, but she also felt a sense of gratitude for the time they had shared together. She knew she had to respect Sofia's decision, no matter how much it hurt. As the plane took off, she looked out the window, her heart heavy with the memories of their Spanish fling, her mind filled with the uncertainty of what the future held.

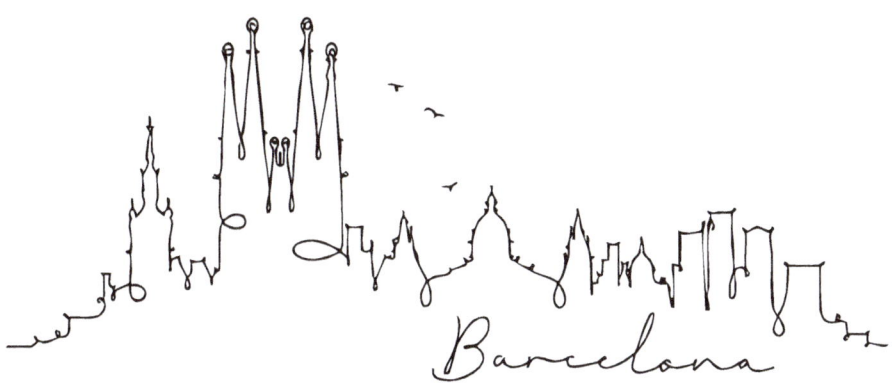

Chapter 18

Choosing to keep a beautiful new friendship

───⋄♥⋄───

Zoe lay in her bed, clutching Maxie tightly against her chest as tears streamed down her face. The familiar weight of her emotions crashed over her like a tidal wave, each sob echoing as she questioned the feeling of heartbreak of her recent trip to Barcelona. She felt raw, exposed, and utterly vulnerable, the memories of Sofia flooding her mind… a whirlwind of laughter, passion, and the bittersweet reality of their fleeting connection.

The first day back home was a blur of emotions, a haze of sadness that enveloped her. She allowed herself to cry, to feel every pang of loss that surged through her. Memories of their intimate moments played on repeat in her mind, the laughter they shared, the way Sofia had looked at her with such intensity, and the warmth of their bodies intertwined. It all felt so real, yet now it was slipping through her fingers like sand.

As the night went on and, many attempted phone calls from friends and little short interactions with Ellie throughout the day as Ellie checked on Zoe. Chloe and Ellie wanted to know all the details and, how Zoe felt and what sounded like a magical romantic dream trip. She explained at first, she just needed some time alone after processing her feelings. Zoe finally started to breathe. She realized that the moment with Sofia was just that—a moment. A beautiful life experience that opened her heart again, but it wasn't love. It was a shared connection that she was grateful for, one that had taught her about herself and her capacity for intimacy.

Zoe sat up, wiping her tears away with the back of her hand. Maxie looked up at her, her big brown eyes filled with concern. "I know, buddy," she whispered, scratching behind his ears. "It hurts, but I'll be okay." She took a deep breath, trying to shake off the heaviness that clung to her.

The next day, Zoe picked up her phone and dialed Sofia's number. Her heart raced as she waited for the call to connect. What would she say? How could she express the whirlwind of emotions that had consumed her since their time together? But as Sofia's voice filled her ear, Zoe felt a sense of calm wash over her.

"Hey, Zoe," Sofia said, her tone warm yet cautious. "How are you?"

"I'm okay, I think," Zoe replied, her voice wavering slightly. "I just wanted to talk. I know we agreed to be friends, but I needed to hear your voice."

Sofia sighed softly. "I miss you, Zoe. I really do. I'm sorry I have been so busy this week."

Zoe nodded, even though Sofia couldn't see her. "I get it. I just wanted to say that I'm grateful for the time we had together. You opened my heart in ways I didn't expect. I felt more open and vulnerable than I thought I could be. Especially after that sound bath spiritual experience, I went through right before meeting you, and I think I understand it all more now. You are important to me. And being with you showed me I can feel open and enjoy intimacy again."

"And honestly, I think you opened my heart too," Sofia replied, her voice thick with emotion. "I'm glad we met, even if it was just for a short time. I'll always cherish those memories."

As they continued to talk, Zoe felt a sense of relief wash over her. It wasn't the end she had envisioned, but it was a new beginning—a chance to build a friendship that could withstand the distance. They agreed to check in with each other regularly, to support one another from afar, and to cherish the bond they had formed.

After hanging up, Zoe felt lighter, as if a weight had been lifted off her shoulders. She knew that healing would take time, but she was ready to embrace the journey ahead.

Over the next few days, Zoe focused on herself. She spent time with Maxie, taking her on long walks through the park, allowing the fresh air to clear her mind. She reconnected with her friends, sharing stories and laughter, leaning on their support as she navigated her feelings.

Kris was a constant source of comfort, always ready with a sarcastic remark to lighten the mood. "You know, Zoe, it's just a fling. You've had plenty of those," he said one evening as they sat on the couch, sipping wine. "You'll find someone who makes you feel even better and is ready for more. Trust me."

Charlie and Leo joined them, bringing their infectious energy and humor. "Let's plan a night out," Leo suggested as he air dances a little. "We'll hit the town and dance until you forget all about your Spanish fling woman."

Zoe laughed, appreciating their efforts to lift her spirits. "Okay, but only if you promise to take me to Flicks. You know it's my fav."

As the days turned into weeks, Zoe began to feel more like herself again. She started applying for remote jobs, exploring opportunities that would allow her to work from anywhere. The idea of moving somewhere new excited her, igniting a spark of hope within her.

Meanwhile, she kept in touch with Sofia, their conversations becoming a source of comfort in her life. They shared updates about their days, their dreams, and the little moments that made them smile. Zoe found solace in knowing that Sofia was still a part of her life, even if it wasn't the way she had initially imagined.

One evening, as Zoe sat at her desk, her laptop open in front of her, she received a message from Sofia. "Hey, just checking in! How's life treating you?"

Zoe smiled, her heart warming at the familiar exchange. "Hey! It's going well. Just applying for jobs and trying to figure out my next steps. I think I'm still hoping to travel more, so I am applying for remote jobs as well so I can be flexible. You know, maybe work from anywhere. Anyway, so many possibilities. How about you?"

Sofia replied almost instantly, "Same here! Just working at the café and trying to stay busy. I've been thinking about you."

Zoe's heart fluttered at the words. "I've been thinking about you too. I hope you're taking care of yourself."

As they continued to chat, Zoe felt a sense of connection that transcended distance. They were building a friendship rooted in understanding and support, and for the first time since returning home, Zoe felt a sense of peace.

Days turned into weeks, and Zoe found herself embracing the uncertainty of life. She was learning to navigate her emotions, to honor her experiences, and to cherish the connections she had formed.

And so, with each passing day, Zoe healed a little more. She learned to appreciate the beauty of her time with Sofia, recognizing it as a valuable chapter in her life. It was a reminder that love comes in many forms, and sometimes, the most profound connections can blossom in unexpected ways.

As she scrolled through job listings, her mind racing with possibilities, Zoe felt a renewed sense of purpose. She was ready to embrace whatever adventures awaited her, to step into the unknown with an open heart, and to continue writing her story—one filled with love, laughter, and the promise of new beginnings.

Chapter 19

Finding a way back to Barcelona round 2

♡♥♡

Zoe stood in her small kitchen, the aroma of freshly brewed coffee wafting through the air as she stared at her laptop screen. The email notification had come in just moments ago, and her heart raced as she read the subject line: "Interview for Remote Position." She could hardly believe it. After weeks of searching, she had finally landed a remote job that would allow her to travel, work, and experience life in a way she had only dreamed of.

"Maxie, can you believe it?" she exclaimed, her voice filled with excitement as she turned to her dog, who wagged his tail in response. "This could be my chance to live anywhere, even in Europe!"

As she read through the details of the job, Zoe felt a mix of exhilaration and apprehension. The position would last for three months, allowing her the flexibility to work from anywhere, and she could potentially return to Barcelona—back to have more chances to travel and maybe even see

Sofia more. The thought sent a thrill through her, but it was accompanied by a wave of uncertainty. What would it mean for her relationship with Sofia? Were they ready to explore that connection further, or would it complicate things?

Zoe took a deep breath, her mind racing with possibilities. She knew she had to share the news with Sofia first. Picking up her phone, she quickly typed out a message, her fingers trembling with anticipation.

"Hey, Sofia! I just got an offer for a remote job! I could potentially come back to Barcelona for three months! Or just anywhere, somewhere in Europe, would be a dream. I would like to start somewhere familiar, and it was really beautiful there. How crazy is this, though?"

The response came almost instantly. "OMG! That's incredible, Zoe! You should come back! We can explore the city together, and I can show you my favorite spots. Are you serious? I'm so happy for you, amazing."

Zoe's heart soared at Sofia's enthusiasm. "Yes! I'm serious! I can't believe this is happening. But I'm also nervous about what it means for us. You know I'm not trying to come back just for you or put pressure on you."

Sofia's reply was quick. "Let's not overthink it. We can take it one day at a time. I'd love to have you around, and we can see where it leads."

Zoe felt a rush of warmth at Sofia's words. She wanted to believe that this could be a new chapter for them, one filled with adventure and deeper connection. But as she put her phone down, the weight of reality began to settle in. Was she ready to leave her life behind? Would she be able to step away from the comfort of her routine and embrace the unknown?

Later that evening, Zoe met Ellie for coffee at their favorite café, Amore Coffee. The familiar ambiance wrapped around her like a warm hug, but she couldn't shake the feeling of anxiety that clung to her. As they settled into their seats, Zoe took a deep breath, ready to share her news.

"Ellie, I have something big to tell you," Zoe said, her voice steady but filled with emotion. "I got a remote job offer that would allow me to travel to Europe for three months."

Ellie's eyes widened with excitement. "Zoe, that's amazing! You've been wanting this for so long! Are you going to take it?"

Zoe hesitated, her heart racing. "I want to, but I'm scared. What if I leave everything behind and it doesn't work out? What if I miss home? What if I miss you, I know I'll miss you?"

Ellie reached across the table, squeezing Zoe's hand. "You have to follow your heart. This is your chance to explore to live your dreams. And I'll always be here for you, no matter where you are. Plus, I'll be planning my own adventures with Chloe, so I'll be busy, too. Maybe the timing was all meant to be."

Zoe smiled, appreciating Ellie's support. "But what if I end up moving out of our apartment? What if I don't come back?"

"Zoe, you have to do what feels right for you. If this job and going to Europe is what you want, then go for it. You've been talking about this for over a year about what a dream would be to do something like this. You're not leaving me behind; you're just expanding your horizons. And if you want to come back, you can always find a way to make it work. You have a support system here, and we all support you."

Zoe nodded, feeling a sense of clarity wash over her. Ellie was right. This was an opportunity for growth, for adventure, and she couldn't let fear hold her back. "I think I'm going to do it. I'll take the job, I'll move for 3 months, and see where it leads me."

As they continued to talk, Zoe felt a sense of excitement bubbling within her. The prospect of traveling to Barcelona of reconnecting with Sofia filled her with hope. She was ready to embrace the unknown, to step into this new chapter of her life.

Later that night, Zoe sat on her bed, her laptop open in front of her. She drafted an email accepting the job offer, her heart racing with anticipation. As she hit send, she felt a rush of exhilaration wash over her.

"Maxie, I'm going on an adventure!" she exclaimed, pulling the dog into her arms. "I can't wait to see where this journey takes me."

In the days that followed, Zoe began to prepare for her upcoming move. She started packing her things sorting through her belongings to decide what to take with her. Each item brought back memories, and as she reminisced, she felt a mix of nostalgia and excitement.

She also kept in touch with Sofia, their conversations filled with playful banter and anticipation. "I can't wait for you to come back," Sofia would say, her voice laced with excitement. "We'll make the most of your time here. You'll finally get to see Europe more, and I'll have another friend here."

As she stood at the crossroads of change, Zoe felt a sense of empowerment wash over her. She was ready to embrace the unknown, to follow her heart, and to see where this journey would lead. With each step forward, she knew she was not just chasing dreams; she was creating a life filled with chance, love, laughter, and the promise of new beginnings. Zoe starts to tell her family and friends more and more every day about her decision and plans for the departure.

Chapter 20

The Farewell Symphony
"End Of An Era"

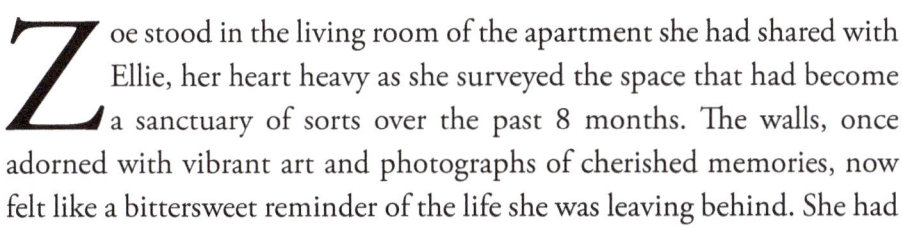

Zoe stood in the living room of the apartment she had shared with Ellie, her heart heavy as she surveyed the space that had become a sanctuary of sorts over the past 8 months. The walls, once adorned with vibrant art and photographs of cherished memories, now felt like a bittersweet reminder of the life she was leaving behind. She had made the decision to move out, to embrace the unknown, and take a leap of faith as she prepared for her upcoming adventure in Barcelona.

"Are you sure about this?" Ellie's voice broke through Zoe's thoughts, her expression a mix of concern and support. She leaned against the doorframe, arms crossed, watching Zoe with a mixture of admiration and worry.

Zoe took a deep breath, her heart racing. "Yeah, I think it's for the best. I need to clear my head, and moving to my mom's for now feels like the right choice. I'll be a nomad for a bit, and who knows what will happen in Barcelona?"

Ellie nodded, though Zoe could see the uncertainty in her eyes. "I get it. But it's still a big change. Are you sure you want to leave this place vs just leaving for a few months and coming back? We've built so many memories here."

Zoe smiled softly, her heart aching at the thought of leaving. "I know, and I'll always cherish those memories. But I think it's time for a new chapter. Financially, it makes more sense, too. We can still stay close, and I'll come back to visit. Plus, you and Chloe are planning to move in together, right?"

"Yeah," Ellie replied, her tone brightening slightly. "We've been talking about it more. It feels right, and it's exciting to think about building a new life together."

Zoe felt a rush of happiness for her friend. "That's amazing, Ellie. You deserve all the happiness in the world." She stepped forward, pulling Ellie into a tight hug. "Thank you for being so supportive. I couldn't have done any of this without you."

As they pulled away, Zoe felt a sense of finality wash over her. She had spent countless nights laughing, singing songs while Ellie played piano, and dreaming about the future in this apartment, and now it was time to say goodbye. She glanced around the room one last time, her heart heavy yet hopeful.

After a few hours of packing and sorting through her belongings, Zoe had managed to downsize her life into a few boxes. She had decided to leave behind most of her furniture, opting to keep only a few sentimental items and her dad's pickup truck, which she planned to leave at her mom's house.

"Are you ready?" Ellie asked, breaking the silence as Zoe finished packing the last of her things.

"Almost," Zoe replied, her voice steady.

As they made their way to the door, Zoe felt a mix of excitement and sadness. She had planned a small farewell gathering with her friends that evening, a chance to celebrate the memories they had shared and the new adventures that lay ahead.

Later that night, the apartment was filled with laughter and love as Zoe's friends gathered to bid her farewell. Kris, Charlie, Leo, Parker, London, and Annabella all crammed into the living room, their energy infectious.

"Zoe! We're going to miss you so much!" Annabella exclaimed, her arms wide open as she enveloped Zoe in a tight hug. "You better come back and visit us! Also, send us so many postcards."

"I promise I will, or you come visit me, I'd love that," Zoe replied, her heart swelling with gratitude. "You all mean the world to me."

As the night wore on, they reminisce about their favorite memories with Zoe, sharing stories that made everyone laugh.

"Let's toast to Zoe and her new adventure!" Charlie raised his glass, a mischievous grin on his face. "May she find love, laughter, and plenty of adventures in Barcelona!"

"Cheers!" Everyone echoed, their glasses clinking together as they took a sip.

Zoe felt a rush of warmth as she looked around at her friends, each one holding a special place in her heart. "Thank you all for being here. I couldn't have asked for a better support system. I'm strong and ready because of friends like you."

As the night continued, Zoe felt a sense of peace wash over her. She was ready to embrace the unknown, ready to take a leap of faith into the next chapter of her life.

But just as the laughter began to fill the air again,

Zoe's phone buzzed with a notification. She glanced down, an unexpected message from the girl she had briefly hooked up with before Sofia.

"Hey, Zoe! Adele, I know it's been a while, but I've been thinking about you. Can we talk? I have feelings I want to share before you leave."

Zoe's eyes widened as she read the message, a mix of surprise and confusion flooding her mind. Just when she thought she had closed the door on her past, it seemed to swing back open.

"Everything okay?" Ellie asked, noticing the change in Zoe's expression.

"Uh, yeah," Zoe replied, her voice shaky. "It's just… Adele, remember her? She wants to talk before I leave."

"Are you going to?" Ellie asked, her curiosity piqued.

Zoe hesitated, her mind racing with thoughts. On one hand, she wanted to honor the connection she had with this girl, but on the other hand, she was still navigating her feelings for Sofia. "I don't know. I guess I need to think about it."

"Just invite her over and find out what she wants to say," Ellie suggests.

Zoe felt torn between the past and the future. She had built a connection with Sofia that had opened her heart, but now she was faced with the possibility of mixing feelings or something she thought was closed with this old fling. Zoe invites Adele over and has no expectations. She decides that she's not doing anything wrong, and since Sofia told Zoe she wasn't into having a full-on relationship with her that it's only fair for Zoe to hear Adele out without guilt.

Chapter 21

What has she done? Don't mix the past with your future.

———♥———

Zoe's eyes fluttered open. She turned her head slowly, only to find Adele nestled beside her, her face peaceful and serene. A warm smile over Zoe's face, but it was quickly overshadowed by a rush of guilt that gripped her chest like a vice.

What had she done?

The memories of the night before surged back, each moment vivid and electric. Thoughts of being a little drunk last night but having fun like old times.

"Damn it," Zoe whispered to herself, burying her face in her hands. She had never intended for things to escalate or go this way. Yet, here she was, waking up next to Adele, feeling a mix of confusion and regret. She had wanted to recognize her connection with Sofia, to explore what they had built together over the months. But now, with Adele beside her, she felt as if she had betrayed that connection. Confused why she felt like this.

Zoe slipped out of bed, careful not to disturb Adele. She tiptoed quietly to the bathroom, splashing cold water on her face in an attempt to shake off the slight hangover. As she stared at her reflection in the mirror, she couldn't help but feel the weight of her choices pressing down on her. She had crossed a line, and now she was left grappling with the consequences.

As she brushed her teeth, her phone buzzed on the counter, pulling her attention away from her thoughts. She glanced at the screen to see a message from Sofia, and her heart sank.

"Hey Zoe, just wanted to wish you good luck on the drive to your mom's and with the moving. I hope everything goes smoothly. Miss you!"

Zoe felt a pang of longing mixed with guilt.

She had been ignoring Sofia's texts since their last conversation, giving herself time to process everything.

Sofia had been so sweet, so understanding, but the truth was that she had also made it clear she didn't want a relationship right now.

And here she was, tangled up with Adele, who had made her feelings crystal clear.

She leaned against the bathroom counter, her mind racing. Should she respond? Should she tell Sofia about Adele? Would that even matter? Zoe knew she needed to gather her thoughts before making any decisions. The last thing she wanted was to hurt Sofia, but she also couldn't ignore her mixed feelings for Adele.

Just then, she heard Adele stirring in bed, her voice soft and slightly groggy. "Zoe? Are you okay?"

Zoe took a deep breath and stepped back into the bedroom, forcing a smile. "Yeah, I'm good. Just… getting ready for the day."

Adele propped herself up on one elbow, her hair wild. "You look a bit pale. Did you sleep okay?"

Zoe nodded, though it felt like a lie. "I did. Just a lot on my mind, I guess."

Adele's eyes softened with concern. "Do you want to talk about it? I mean, we did have quite the night. And I know you are leaving."

Zoe's mind raced at the thought of laying everything out on the table. She wanted to be honest, but the fear of hurting Adele was overwhelming. "I think we need to talk, yeah. About… everything."

Adele sat up fully, her expression shifting to one of seriousness. "Okay. I'm here for it. Whatever you need to say."

Zoe took a seat on the edge of the bed, her hands clasped tightly in her lap. "Last night was unexpected for me. I didn't plan on it happening, and I'm still trying to figure out what it means."

Adele nodded, her gaze steady and unwavering. "I get that. I spent a long time thinking about how I felt about you, even when we weren't together. I regret not telling you sooner, and I don't want to hide my feelings anymore."

Zoe felt a rush of emotions. Adele was brave, and that was something she admired. But the weight of her own feelings was heavy. "I care about you, Adele. I really do. But I can't shake this guilt I feel about Sofia, you know that's who's there in Barcelona. We had something special, and I didn't want to hurt her. Especially if I'm going back soon and could explore more feelings with her again."

Adele's expression softened, and she reached out to touch Zoe's hand. "You don't have to feel guilty for exploring your feelings. You deserve to find happiness, and if that means taking time to figure things out with Sofia or with me, then that's okay. Just know that I'm not going anywhere."

Zoe felt a flicker of hope at Adele's words, but uncertainty still lingered. "But Sofia is so sweet. She's been nothing but honest with me, and I don't want to lead her on if I am holding on to mixed feelings. She told me she didn't want a relationship, but right now, I'm here, and I've started something with you again."

Adele's brows furrowed slightly. "What do you want, Zoe? That's what matters most. If you feel something for Sofia, then you should explore that. But if you feel drawn to me, then we can figure it out together."

Zoe took a deep breath, her heart racing. "I don't know. I feel like I'm being pulled in two different directions. Sofia is in Spain, and we've had this beautiful connection, but she's also made it clear that she's not ready for anything serious. And then there's you, right here, even though I'm leaving, you're saying you're here and you want this."

Adele smiled softly, her thumb brushing over Zoe's knuckles. "I'm willing to wait for you, Zoe. I want you to take your time and figure out what you really want. Just know that I'm here, and I'm not going to give up on us."

Zoe felt a rush of warmth at Adele's words, a sense of comfort in the chaos. "Thank you for being so understanding. I really appreciate it. I just need to think things through."

Adele nodded, her expression encouraging. "Take all the time you need. I'll be here when you're ready."

Zoe felt a sense of relief washes over her, but the guilt still lingered. She needed to find a way to balance her feelings for both women to honor the connections she had forged. As she stood up to gather her things for the move, she felt a renewed sense of determination.

"Alright, I guess I should get going. I have a lot to do today," Zoe said, trying to shake off the heavy emotions.

Adele smiled. "I'll help you."

As they began to pack up Zoe's things, the air was filled with a mix of laughter and lighthearted banter. Zoe felt grateful for Adele's presence. The way she made the chaos of moving feel a little less overwhelming. But in the back of her mind, the weight of her choices still loomed large.

Once they finished packing the car, Zoe took a moment to gather her thoughts before hitting the road. She pulled out her phone, hesitating for a moment before typing a response to Sofia's message.

"Thanks, Sofia! I really appreciate it. I miss you too. I'll text you when I make it to my mom's safely."

As she hit send, she felt a sense of finality. It was a small step, but it felt significant. She was acknowledging her feelings for both women, and she was ready to embrace whatever came next.

With Adele by her side, Zoe climbed into the driver's seat, the engine humming to life. She took a deep breath, feeling a mix of excitement and apprehension as she turned to Adele, who was hanging through her truck window. "Bye Adele!"

Adele sighed, "Call me when you get there, okay? I'll miss you."

Chapter 22

More women, more conversations

———————❤———————

Zoe's pickup truck rumbled down the familiar street leading to her mom's house, the landscape a comforting blend of nostalgia and anticipation. The week ahead was a swirl of emotions: excitement for her upcoming adventure in Barcelona, confusion about her feelings for Adele and Sofia, and a lingering sense of uncertainty about what the next 3 months and future ahead. As she pulled up to the cozy house nestled among the trees, she felt a mix of relief and apprehension.

Her mom greeted her with a warm embrace, the familiar scent of home enveloping her. "Zoe, it's so good to have you back," her mom said, her eyes shining with happiness. "I've missed you."

"I've missed you too, Mom," Zoe replied, her voice tinged with emotion. "It's good to be home."

As the days passed, Zoe found herself lost in a whirlwind of preparations for her trip. She sorted through her belongings, packed her suitcase, and spent quality time with her mom. But amidst the busyness, her mind was a tangled web of thoughts and feelings.

She couldn't shake the guilt she felt about Adele, nor could she ignore the longing she had for Sofia. How did this happen? What will she do? Why is this happening right now? What does this all mean? Do I have feelings again for someone? Do I like Sofia more than I admit? Do I like the attention from Adele? All these thoughts running through Zoe's head.

One evening, as Zoe sat on the porch, watching the sunset paint the sky in hues of orange and pink, she heard the crunch of gravel under tires. She turned to see a familiar car pulling up the driveway, and her heart leapt into her throat. Adele stepped out, her eyes filled with a mix of determination and persuasion.

"Adele? What are you doing here?" Zoe asked, her voice barely above a whisper.

Adele walked toward her, her steps steady and sure. "I couldn't stay away, Zoe. I missed you too much. I had to see you before you leave."

Zoe felt a rush of emotions…surprise, confusion, and a flicker of desire. "Adele, I… I don't know what to say."

Adele reached out, taking Zoe's hand in hers. "You don't have to say anything. Just be with me. Let's not think about the future or the past. Just be here, with me, now."

Zoe felt torn, her heart pulling her in different directions. But in that moment, she couldn't deny the connection she felt with Adele. She nodded, her voice soft. "Okay."

They went to a local bar to hang out. They spent the evening talking and laughing. The chemistry between them was nostalgic and familiar. As the night wore on, they found themselves drawn to each other, their bodies moving in sync as they made their way to a nearby hotel.

The room was dimly lit, the air charged with anticipation.

Adele's lips found Zoe's, their kiss passionate and slow. Zoe's hands explored Adele's body, turning her on. They moved together till Adele led Zoe to the bed. Zoe started sliding her fingers over Adele's clit and started to rub it slowly. Zoe noticed Adele's urge to get Zoe's long fingers inside of her as fast as she could and started pressing her fingers into her pussy. Zoe started to thrust her arm and fingers more and more and listened to Adele enjoying the pleasure. But as the night wore on, Zoe felt a growing sense of unease.

She couldn't shake the feeling that something was off, that the connection she had felt with Adele was fading.

Adele, though, was feeling the best sex of her life, the way they were moving together. Adele was breathing heavily and was moaning with pleasure, her body responding to every touch. Zoe was trying to stay present, but she knew that this wasn't what she wanted. She wanted Sofia.

As they lay entwined in the aftermath, Zoe felt a profound sense of clarity wash over her. She knew what she had to do. She turned to Adele, her heart heavy with the weight of her decision.

"Adele, I can't do this," Zoe said softly, her voice filled with regret. "I care about you, but I can't be with you. Not like this."

Adele's eyes widened with surprise and hurt. "Zoe, what are you saying? What was that then? Why are you doing this? I thought we had something."

Zoe took a deep breath, her heart aching. "We did, Adele. But ugh, girl, I can't ignore my feelings for Sofia. I need to be honest with myself and with you. I'm sorry."

Adele's expression shifted to one of understanding, though the pain was still apparent in her eyes. "I get it, Zoe. I just wish things could be different."

Zoe felt gratitude for Adele's understanding. "Me too. But I have to follow my gut, or heart, whatever this is."

As they said their goodbyes, Zoe felt relieved and hopeful. She knew she had made the right decision, even if it was painful. She drove back to her mom's house, her mind racing with thoughts of Sofia. She needed to talk to her, to confess everything, and see where they stood.

Later that night, Zoe dialed Sofia's number, her heart pounding in her chest. She wanted it to be super real and personal for such a more serious conservation. So Zoe decided it was best to video call. As the video chat connected, she felt a rush of excitement and anxiety. But when the screen flickered to life, Zoe's stomach sank. Instead of Sofia's face, she saw a woman she didn't recognize, a beautiful woman with dark hair and piercing hazel eyes.

"Hola?" the woman said, her voice laced with curiosity.

Zoe felt a wave of confusion and shock. Her eyes widened. "Um, hola. Is Sofia there?"

The woman's expression shifted to one of realization. "Ah, you must be Zoe. I'm Neila, Sofia's… uhh friend. She's in the shower right now. Can I take a message?"

Zoe felt a pang of jealousy, though she knew she had no right to feel that way. "Uh, no, that's okay. I'll call back later."

As she hung up the phone, Zoe felt a mix of emotions swirling within her. She had no right to be mad or jealous, but the sight of Neila answering Sofia's phone had shaken her. She clearly remembered that name, Neila. Neila, who was that again to Sofia? Zoe filters through conversations in her mind, trying to connect the dots and if Sofia mentioned her recently as Neila was Sofia's Ex-girlfriend, whom she said was over and broken up months ago. When did Neila return to Sofia's life? Why didn't she mention that? What is she doing back in her apartment? Why is she answering her phone? How did she know Zoe's name? She knew she and Sofia had some talking and explaining to do.

With a heavy heart, Zoe lay in bed, her mind racing with thoughts of Sofia and the unknown future. She knew she had to be honest, to lay everything on the table.. But for now, she needed to gather her thoughts and prepare for the conversation that could change everything.

As she tried to sleep, Zoe knew that the coming days would be a whirlwind of emotions. But she was ready to face whatever came her way, to deal with all of it.

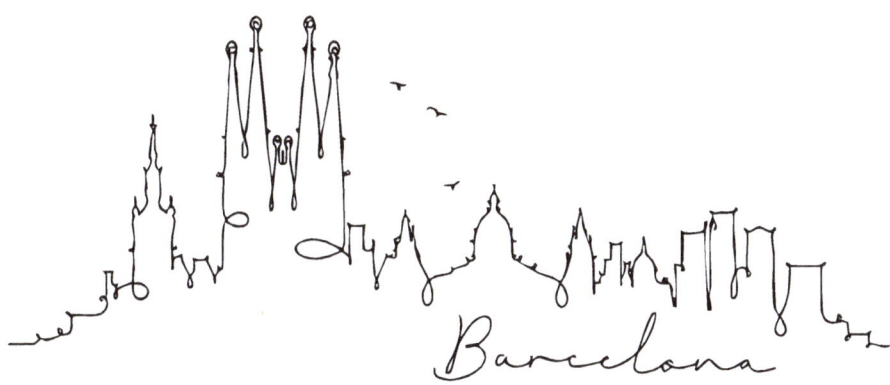

Chapter 23

Confessions of the Past

Z oe woke up with a start, her heart pounding in her chest. She had tossed and turned all night, her dreams haunted by the image of Neila answering Sofia's phone. She knew she had to talk to Sofia to clear the air and confess her own transgressions. She dialed Sofia's number, her hands shaking slightly as she waited for the call to connect.

Sofia answered, her voice warm but cautious. "Hey, Zoe."

Zoe took a deep breath, steeling herself for the conversation ahead. "Hey, Sofia. I think we need to talk."

There was a pause on the other end, a soft intake of breath. "Yeah, I think we do," Sofia replied, her voice steady.

Zoe started to pace around her room, her nerves getting the better of her. "So, last night, I called you. And a woman answered your phone. Neila, right?"

Sofia sighed, a sound that was part resignation, part relief. With a little bit of laughter but hesitation, "Yes, that was Neila. She's… she's my ex-girlfriend. But it's not what you think, Zoe."

Zoe felt a tiny bit of worry and jealousy, but she pushed it down, trying to keep an open mind. "Okay, so what is it then? You can tell me if you feel comfortable; I'm not going to judge you."

Sofia explained, her voice filled with honesty.

"Neila and I used to live together. We broke up months ago, as I mentioned, but we're still on the same lease for this apartment. She stays here sometimes because she has nowhere else to go. But I promise you, Zoe, there's nothing going on between us. I have no reason to hide anything from you. We're just friends now. I know I don't owe you this information but I wanted to tell you. I was going to tell you before you found out like this. Now you understand more why I'm not so ready for anything more relationship-wise as well…I'm aware I need more time, independence, etc."

"Friends who live together?" Zoe asked, almost with a sigh and fake laughter.

"Friends who are stuck in a lease together, it's complicated and annoying I know. But nothing is happening between us." Zoe could hear the sincerity in Sofia's voice, and she chose to believe her. "I understand, Sofia. It's a complicated situation. Thank you for being honest with me, girl. I was definitely in shock. Not mad. Just started to wonder. However, it's nice to talk to you about it."

Sofia let out a breath, a sound of relief. "Thank you for understanding, Zoe. I know it's a lot to take in."

Zoe shifted her body around on the other line. Even though Sofia couldn't see her, she nodded. "It is, but I get it. Life is messy sometimes." She took a deep breath, knowing it was her turn to confess. "But I have something to tell you, too. It's for some reason kinda hard for me, so bare with me."

There was a pause, a moment of silence that felt heavy with anticipation. "What is it, Zoe?" Sofia asked, her voice soft and curious.

Zoe took a deep breath, her heart racing. "Remember Adele? The girl I told you about, the one I had a brief thing with before you and I started talking?"

"Yeah, I remember," Sofia replied.

Zoe felt a rush of nerves, but she pushed through. "Well, she came back into my life recently. And... and we slept together. I got caught up in the moment, and I'm so sorry, Sofia. I should have told you sooner. She's been with me all week. I know we aren't a thing, and I don't owe you anything, either. However, it was going to eat me up inside if I didn't tell you before coming back to Barcelona and seeing you."

There was a long pause, a silence that felt deafening. Zoe could almost hear Sofia's thoughts racing. She could almost feel her confusion and hurt. "Why, Zoe?" Sofia finally asked, her voice filled with emotion and confusion as to why she just asked her that so bluntly. "Why did you sleep with her?" The words just come blurting out.

Zoe sighed, trying to find the right words. "I don't know, Sofia. I was confused, and I thought I had feelings for her. But I realized quickly that I didn't. She was persistent in her feelings for me and I was confused about her and my attachment to home or my life here. Then I just honestly I felt no emotional connection. I didn't feel the connection that made me feel like it was right. So, I broke it off with her because I knew it wasn't fair to either of us. And it wasn't fair to you. Not knowing what's been going on with me."

Sofia was quiet for a moment, processing everything. "So, what does this mean, Zoe?" she finally asked, her voice filled with uncertainty.

Zoe felt a rush of emotions, a mix of fear and hope. "I don't know, Sofia. I just know that I can't ignore my feelings for you. I want to be honest with you, even if it's hard. Even if it hurts. I don't know why I feel drawn to you and the need to be honest with you. I guess because of the connection we had already, and might have something more. Felt weird that I was intimate again with someone else, I don't know. Okay, I'll shut up now, I just needed to confess this to you."

Sofia was silent for a moment before she spoke, her voice soft. "I appreciate your honesty, Zoe. And I understand. We both have pasts, and we both have baggage. Maybe this is a chance for us to be open with each other."

Zoe felt a rush of relief wash over her. "I'd like that, Sofia. I want to be open with you. I want to get to know you more and build on our new formed friendship."

As they continued to talk, Zoe and Sofia found themselves bonding over their shared experiences, their past mistakes, and their hopes for the future. They laughed about their ex-girlfriends, sharing stories of bad dates and awkward encounters.

"Remember that girl I told you about, the one who brought her mom on our first date?" Sofia said, her voice filled with laughter.

Zoe chuckled, the sound warm and genuine. "Oh my God, yes! That's hilarious. I once went on a date with a girl who spent the entire time talking about her ex and their dog, that they have shared custody with. It was so awkward."

They shared more stories, their laughter filling the air as they reminisced about their past experiences.

It felt cathartic, a chance to heal and move forward together.

As the conversation wound down, Zoe felt a sense of hope and comfortability. She and Sofia had weathered the storm, had faced their pasts, and were ready to build whatever kinda relationship they were about to get into.

"So, what now?" Zoe asked, her voice soft.

Sofia smiled, her voice filled with warmth. "Now, we take it one day at a time. We just be honest with each other, and we see where this journey takes us. I'll see you in a few days, yes?"

Zoe nodded on her end with a smile and a feeling of peace in her heart. "I'd like that, Sofia. I'd like that very much."

And with that, they said their goodbyes, their hearts filled with hope and the promise of new beginnings. As Zoe hung up the phone, she felt a sense of clarity. She was ready to embrace the unknown, to step into the future with an open heart, and to see where her journey with Sofia would lead.

As she sat on her bed later that night, her fingers dancing over the strings of her guitar, she began to write a new song. A song about love, about healing, and about the beauty of second chances. She would be traveling to Barcelona soon, and she wanted to be able to play it for Sofia. She knew she would be nervous, but she would do it. As she sang the first few lines, she felt excited and eager to explore. " I never knew when and where I would find you. There you were on the other side of the phone. Come on, girl, tell me you wanna see me. One long flight, baby, and I'll be knocking on your door…" Zoe whispers the song to herself.

Meanwhile, Zoe kept in touch with her friends, sharing updates about her upcoming trip and her conversations with Sofia. They were all supportive, offering words of encouragement and excitement. Also making sure she keeps two feet on the floor so she doesn't float away too quickly on the "drunk in love" movement of Sofia.

"You deserve this, Zoe," Ellie said one evening as she sat on the porch, watching the sunset on the phone with her. "You deserve to find love and happiness, wherever that may be."

Zoe smiled through the phone, feeling grateful for her friend's support. "Thank you, Ellie. I couldn't do any of this without you."

Chapter 24

Zoe moves to BCN!
Phase 1

Z oe said goodbye to her mom and made sure her room at her mom's house was all packed up and organized for her when she returns. Zoe said goodbye to the life she knew well.

The day has come!

Zoe stood in the airport, her heart pounding with a mix of excitement and nerves. She had been dreaming of this moment for weeks, and now it was finally here.

She was moving to Barcelona for three months, ready to embrace the unknown with her new job and see where her connection with Sofia would lead. As she boarded the plane, she felt a rush of anticipation wash over her.

Throughout the flight, Zoe and Sofia exchanged excited messages, keeping the conversation light and casual. They talked about their plans for the week when Sofia wasn't working. Zoe felt a sense of comfort in their easy banter, a reminder of the connection they had built over the past months. Talking about how many new inside jokes were probably about to happen.

As the plane touched down in Barcelona, Zoe felt a surge of adrenaline. She was here, in a new country that she loved already, ready to embrace whatever came her way. The city was glowing as she stepped out of the airport, taking a deep breath of the fresh air.

Sofia was waiting outside for her at her new flat apartment, her eyes shining with excitement. As Zoe walked through the door, Sofia immediately pulled her into a tight hug, their bodies melting together in a familiar embrace. "I'm so happy you're here," Sofia whispered, her voice filled with warmth.

"Me too," Zoe replied, her heart swelling with happiness. "I can't believe I'm finally back."

They spent the evening catching up, their laughter filling the room as they shared stories and reminisced about their past adventures. As the night wore on, they found themselves drawn to each other, their bodies moving in sync, and started to get tingles again. Should they hook up? Zoe wanted to respect the friendship level of their relationship they shifted to over the month. Now, in person, it might be hard to deny themselves. They kept their desires in check.

The next evening, they met for vermouth & olives at a quaint little tapas place called Coco Rita near Zoe's new flat. As they sat down, Zoe felt a rush of affection wash over her. She reached out, taking Sofia's hand in hers, their fingers entwining naturally.

"I've missed this," Zoe said softly, her voice filled with emotion. "I've missed you."

Sofia smiled, her eyes shining with happiness. "I've missed you too, Zoe. More than you know."

Zoe, excited and surprised, replied, "Really?".

As they sipped their vermouth, and twirled their olives on a toothpick in their mouths slowly while looking at each other, they couldn't ignore the spark between them. Their eyes met, and at that moment, they both knew what was about to happen. They made their way back to Zoe's flat, their hearts racing with anticipation.

Their first encounter was shy and nervous, their bodies moving tentatively as they rediscovered each other. Taking things really slow this time. Eyes locked in an intense passion and stare of wondering what the other was thinking. Zoe is still a little cautious.

But as the days passed, their passion grew more intense, their connection deepening with each moment. They spent the night together for a few days now without having sex.

Lost in the moment one night, it got heated with touch and soft comfort between each other. Zoe's hands slowly touching Sofia's arms and slide to her shoulders and neck. Zoe kisses Sofia softly on the shoulder, and immediately after, Sofia flips herself on top of Zoe, looks at her, and then looks down at her kips. Sofia hovers over Zoe's lips for a few seconds to see if it is okay to kiss her. Zoe holds that moment and doesn't reach up for her lips but gives an exhale and deep look at Sofia and also, looking at her lips, they wait out the sexy moment of anticipation. Sofia kisses Zoe softly and feels Zoe respond and kiss her back as if it were their first and last kiss!

They start to kiss with their tongue and move their hands over each other. Sofia says to Zoe, "We should take this off," as she pulls up Zoe's shirt. Zoe nods and takes off Sofia's shirt as well and then hears a exhale from Sofia, and she bites her lips and says to Zoe, " I've fucking missed your boobs so much. I love your boobs. So sexy." Sofia says as she starts to kiss her nipples. Zoe starts to do the same to Sofia, kissing her neck and slowly slides her hands to her butt over her jeans, and as she does that, Sofia then says, "fuck it, let's take these off too, should we?."

"Yes, baby girl, we should," Zoe says as she unbuttons her jeans and slides them off with the underwear as well without waiting time and another step. Sofia exhilaratingly says, "Yes, I want to feel you on me." They start to wrap their legs tightly around each other, and they start to slide into a spot where they both feel their (v)girls throbbing and clit stimulated. As their "girls" kiss and start to feel more turned on, they flip around, and Zoe gets on top of Sofia. Zoe's fingers start to play around on Sofia's lips down on her girl, and then Sofia whispers in Zoe's ears, "Please go in me." Zoe's two fingers, her index and her middle finger, easily slide into Sofia. The build-up was so amazing that Sofia finds herself orgasming quickly and then cuddles up on Zoe's chest and kisses her neck. They fall asleep happy.

A couple of days of this kinda hooking up continues.

On the fifth day of that week, they found themselves lying in bed, their bodies entwined in the aftermath of their lovemaking. Zoe felt a sense of contentment wash over her, but she also knew that they needed to have a serious conversation about their relationship.

"Sofia," Zoe started, her voice soft. "Should we talk about us?"

Sofia nodded, her expression serious. "Yes, maybe, I've been thinking about it too."

Zoe took a deep breath, steeling herself for the conversation ahead. "I care about you, Sofia. I really do. Maybe it's better to know where we stand. I don't want to be in a relationship one day with someone who doesn't want one."

Sofia sighed, running a hand through her hair. "Zoe, I care about you too. But I'm not ready for a serious relationship right now. I need more time. I haven't had much time between my last breakup, and I can't commit too much right now."

Zoe wasn't surprised and understood Sofia's perspective. "I get it, Sofia. And I respect that. But I don't want to just be a weird situationship.

I want to take things slow, to date you properly, ya know? To go on cute dates and see where this leads. Not as girlfriends or anything. Just date. And I want to be okay with sleeping together and seeing how it goes."

Sofia smiled, her eyes filled with gratitude. "I'd like that, Zoe. I want to take things slow, too. Let's just enjoy each other's company and see where this journey takes us."

Zoe felt a rush of relief wash over her. "Okay. Let's do that. One date at a time, girl."

As they continued to talk, Zoe felt a sense of hope and excitement for the future. She was ready to embrace this new chapter of her life, to explore her connection with Sofia, and to see where their journey would lead.

Later that week, Zoe met her new flat neighbors, Nicolas and Izzy, who were out of town when Zoe first arrived. They were both from the USA and had been living in Barcelona for a few years. They were warm and welcoming, their energy infectious.

"Zoe, it's so great to finally meet you!" Izzy exclaimed, pulling her into a tight hug. "We've heard so much about you from the property manager."

Nicolas nodded in agreement, his smile genuine. "Yeah, we're really excited to have you here. Let us know if you need anything. We think you're going to love Barcelona."

Zoe felt a rush of gratitude for their warmth and kindness. "Thank you both. I'm really excited to be here, too. And I'm looking forward to getting to know you both better."

As the days turned into weeks, Zoe found herself settling into her new life in Barcelona. She explored the city with Sofia, their days filled with laughter, and starting to be a local together. They went on cute dates, their connection deepening with each passing moment. And as they continued to navigate their relationship, Zoe felt a sense of hope and excitement for this chapter in her life in Barcelona.

Zoe met a new gay guy friend through Izzy, her neighbor. His name was Amos. Amos's vibe was instantly bestie vibes with Zoe.

Zoe and Amos started grabbing brunch together every week. Amos was a handsome & wholesome, warm-hearted guy. Super fun having a new gay bestie. Zoe felt like she had a chance at this new city and was slowly building a community there.

One evening, as Zoe sat on the balcony of her flat, watching the sunset paint the sky in hues of orange and pink as her flatmates chattering it up next to her, she felt a profound sense of belonging hit her. She had taken a leap of faith, had stepped into the unknown, and she was grateful for every moment of it. She knew Sofia was the one that brought her there, even though it was an adventure of her own, and she was so thankful. As she took a deep breath, she knew that this was just the beginning of her adventure, and she was ready to see where her journey with Sofia and her new life in Barcelona would lead.

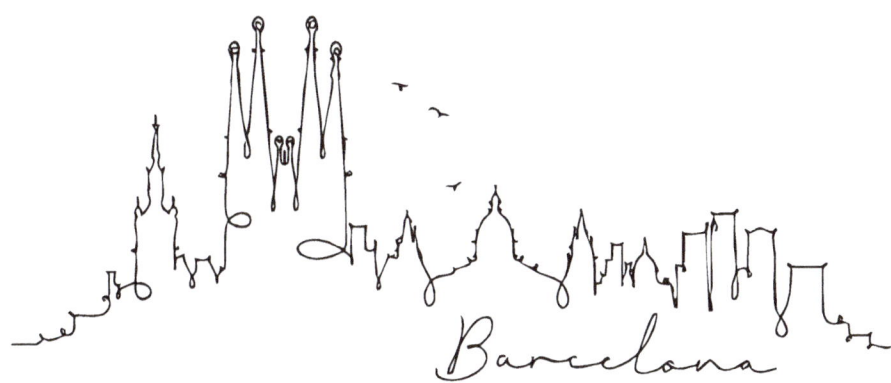

Chapter 25

Unbutting fantasies

———⟡♥⟡———

The warm Barcelona sun-kissed Zoe's skin as she and Sofia wandered through the vibrant streets, their hands entwined and laughter echoing through the air. Their days were filled with adventures and new experiences, each moment deepening their connection. Sofia, ever the enthusiastic tour guide, had planned a day filled with some of Barcelona's most iconic sights.

First on the list was Park Güell. As they climbed the steps to the entrance, Zoe marveled at the colorful mosaics and the whimsical architecture. The park was a feast for the senses, with lush greenery, vibrant colors, and the constant hum of visitors exploring the winding paths. They spent hours wandering, taking in the breathtaking views of the city and stealing kisses behind the columns.

Next, they ventured to Casa Batlló, one of Gaudí's masterpieces. The building's unique facade, with its irregular oval windows and mosaic of broken ceramic tiles, was a sight to behold. Zoe and Sofia explored the interior, marveling at the organic shapes and the play of light and color. They climbed to the roof, where the famous dragon-scale tiles glimmered in the sun, and shared a passionate kiss, the city bustling below them.

As the day turned into evening, they made their way to Tibidabo, the amusement park overlooking Barcelona. The park was a charming mix of vintage rides and modern attractions, offering stunning panoramic views of the city. They rode the Ferris wheel, the city lights twinkling below them, and stole another sweet kiss at the top.

Their nights were filled with even more passion and intimacy. They started spending five nights a week together, their bodies entwined as they explored each other's sexual fantasies.

One night, Sofia suggests that they move the mirror in the room in sight of view for them to watch and stare at each other while having sex. "Look, look how good we look together. Look how sexy you are with me," Sofia says as she's behind Zoe and starts to undress her slowly.

She starts to unbutton her jeans just enough to make her nerves fill with desire. Zoe reaches her arm back and above to touch Sofia's neck. Sofia then unbuttons her blouse one button at a time. As she gets to the last button, she taps Zoe's chin to make sure she watches in the mirror as she opens her shirt and only sees her skin and arms arm her. Sofia takes off the blouse while kissing her shoulder and then, as she grabs her waist, pulls her just a little closer to her. Sofia takes off Zoe's bra and then starts to caress her boobs softly at first, then a little harder before she slides one of her hands down Zoe's unbuttons, flapped open pants, and past her silky black underwear. Zoe starts to touch Sofia's ass as she reaches around and is biting her own lip on how hot it is to watch themselves in the mirror.

Zoe and Sofia get so turned on and start to kiss with Zoe's head tilted back towards Sofia. Zoe turns around and starts to undress Sofia. Then she lifts her up around her curvy body and holds her up on her hips.

She walks forward with Sofia half undressed and lays her on the bed. Sofia is still glancing at the mirror as she loves to see the excitement and fiery turn-on of their bodies together. Zoe starts to kiss Sofia's nipples and abbs and goes towards her underwear on the bottom and pulls off her panties slowly as she slides herself down with the panties and kisses her from hips to toes. As she comes back up she stops just right at Sofia's creases of her hips and inner thighs. Zoe takes one big lick on Sofia's perfect pussy and gets between the lips. Then Zoe just rests her mouth and bottom lip as she takes one big kiss and lets out a sound of enjoyment and signs she finds this taste and moment amazing. She says to Sofia at that moment, " you are so delicious." and before Sofia could say anything back... Zoe puts her two fingers into Sofia's wet vagina, and Sofia just starts moaning and moving around. Sofia grabs Zoe to come up with her to kiss her as she's doing this. They start to flow in rhythm together, and Sofia is telling her in Spanish all the sexy things you can imagine. "Hazme gemir" -"Asi aqui amor"- "Amame salvajemente."

The intensity is driving them both wild. This night was just a build-up of how much their chemistry has continued and keeps growing. They seem to really enjoy each other in and out of the bed!

Zoe visited Sofia at the coffee shop where she worked, watching as she effortlessly charmed customers and crafted beautiful lattes. The café became a second home to Zoe, where she would often set up her laptop and work remotely, stealing glances at Sofia as she worked.

As the weeks passed, Zoe found herself growing more and more busy with her remote job. She loved the work, but it often left her feeling overwhelmed and exhausted. One day, as she was catching up on emails, she received a surprising message from her manager.

"Hey Zoe, we have an upcoming trip to Paris for a team-building event. You'll be joining some of your colleagues who you haven't met before. It's going to be a great opportunity to network and get to know the team better."

Zoe felt a mix of excitement and apprehension. She had always dreamed of visiting Paris, but the thought of meeting new colleagues and navigating a new city was a bit daunting. She quickly replied, confirming her attendance, and began to prepare for the trip.

As she shared the news with Sofia, she noticed a slight shift in Sofia's demeanor. Sofia had always been supportive and encouraging, but there was a hint of something else in her eyes—a flicker of curiosity, perhaps even a touch of concern.

"Nice, who are you going with?" Sofia casually asked as they sat on the balcony of Zoe's flat, sipping wine and watching the sunset.

Zoe shrugged, trying to recall the names from the email. "There's a few people I haven't met before. One of them is a woman named Fallon, pretty sure she's not straight. She's been really talkative and friendly in our group chats. She even texted me personally a few times, just checking in and joking around and sending me memes. She's funny."

Sofia nodded, her expression thoughtful. "That's nice. It's good to make new friends, especially when you're traveling alone."

Zoe watched Sofia closely, trying to gauge her reaction. "Yeah, I guess so. But I'm not really interested in making new friends or anything. I mean, not in that way. You know what I mean?"

Sofia smiled softly, reaching out to take Zoe's hand. "I know, Zoe. I'm not jealous or anything. I just want you to enjoy your trip and make the most of it. If you meet new people and make connections, even flirting, that's amazing. I want you to experience everything Paris has to offer."

Zoe felt a rush of relief wash over her. She knew Sofia was being genuine, and it meant the world to her. "Thank you, Sofia. That means a lot to me. I promise I'm not interested in anyone else. I just want to focus on my work and enjoy the city."

Sofia leaned in, pressing a soft kiss to Zoe's lips. "I know, mi amor. Even if you were, that's okay. You are free to do anything you want. Now, let's talk about something more fun. What do you want to do on our last night together before you leave?"

Zoe grinned, her mind already racing with ideas. "Well, I was thinking we could recreate one of our first date nights. Remember that little tapas bar we went to? We could go there, have some wine, and just enjoy each other's company."

Sofia's eyes lit up with excitement. "I love that idea. Let's do it."

As they made plans for their last night together, Zoe felt a sense of contentment but also a hint of worry and reminders of how casual this relationship, or whatever it is, is. Pushing those inside emotions aside. She was grateful for Sofia's understanding and support, and she was excited for the Weekend adventure that laid ahead in Paris. But for now, she was determined to make the most of her nights in Barcelona with Sofia.

The night before Zoe's departure, they dressed up and headed to the tapas bar, their minds filled with anticipation. The bar was lively and bustling, the air filled with the sound of laughter and the clinking of glasses. They found a cozy corner table, and as they sipped their wine and shared delicious tapas, they reminisced about their time together in Barcelona.

"Remember when we first kissed on the streets?" Sofia asked, her eyes sparkling with amusement.

Zoe laughed, the memory vivid in her mind. "How could I forget? It was so spontaneous and perfect. I felt like I was in a movie. Waiting for a photographer to pop out of nowhere and document the moment, haha."

Sofia grinned, leaning in closer. "You are my movie, beautiful."

As the night wore on, they found themselves lost in each other's company, their connection deepening with each passing moment. They returned to Zoe's flat, their bodies entwined as they made love really passionately as one of their most memorable nights.

The next morning, Zoe woke up early, her nerves hit about traveling. She packed her bags, double-checking to make sure she had everything she needed for her trip to Paris. Sofia helped her, offering words of encouragement and support.

"You're going to have an amazing time, Zoe," Sofia said, pulling her into a tight hug. "I can't wait to hear all about it when you get back. Go have fun."

Zoe felt a lump form in her throat, her emotions threatening to overflow. "I'm going to miss you so much, Sofia. But I promise I'll be back before you know it. What are you going to do this weekend?."

Sofia smiled, her eyes shining with unshed tears. "I know you will. Now go, have an adventure, and come back to me with stories to tell. I'm not sure yet what I'll do, probably call some of my friends and go out."

As Zoe boarded her flight to Paris, she felt a mix of excitement and sadness. She's gonna miss BCN and Sofia and her friends there, even if just for a few days. Now, Zoe and Sofia find out what it's like one weekend apart from each other. Non-committed, but feelings starting to grow.

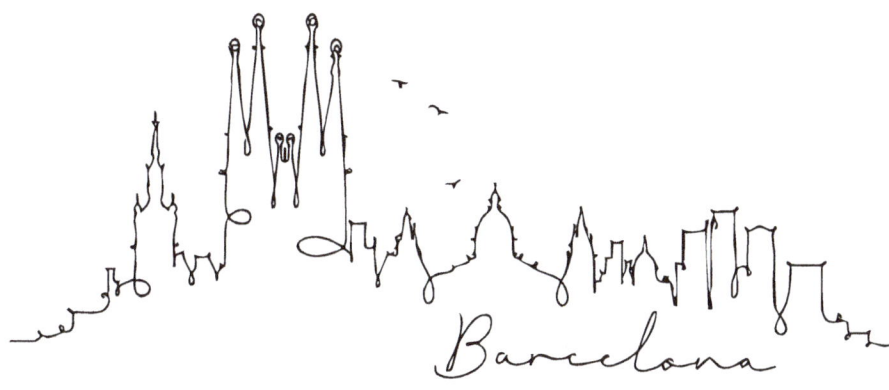

Chapter 26

Guilt in a situationship

———————◦♥◦———————

Sofia glanced at her phone, her eyes widening in surprise. A name she hadn't seen in years flashed across the screen- Lola, a girl she had briefly dated and grew fond of before moving to Barcelona. Lola was in town for the weekend and wanted to catch up. And told Sofia she had something to tell her. Sofia hesitated, her thumbs hovering over the keyboard as she contemplated her response. She finally settled on a casual reply, "Sure, let's meet up. Sounds fun. What did you want to tell me?"

Lola replied that she wanted to pick her brain about something exciting and would tell her when they met up. Sofia mentions to Zoe briefly in a short voice-note she left her, that an old friend of hers is in town and might grab a drink with her. Weirdly hesitant at not mentioning her name.

Meanwhile, in Paris, Zoe was preparing for her work event. She slipped on an elegant black dress, something she only wears for work events or special occasions. She had mentioned Fallon a few times in her texts to Sofia, and she looked forward to meeting the woman who had been so friendly online. She grabbed her phone and sent a quick message to Sofia, "Going for drinks with Fallon after the event. She's been so nice and welcoming. Have fun with your friend!"

Sofia read the message, a small smile playing on her lips. She knew Zoe had no ill intentions, but she also knew that Fallon had been unusually attentive. She pushed the thought aside, focusing instead on her plans with Lola. "Have fun, beautiful," she replied, tucking her phone into her pocket as she left her apartment.

Sofia met Lola at a cozy wine bar, their reunion filled with reminiscing about old times and shared memories. Lola just continued with the stories and caught Sofia up on her life and ordered more wine. One glass of wine turned into two, then three, and before Sofia knew it, she was stumbling back to Lola's hotel room, their bodies pressed tightly together.

As they fell into bed, Sofia's mind flickered with thoughts of Zoe. She pushed them aside, focusing instead on the sensation of Lola's lips on her skin. She was free, she reminded herself, single. But her heart ached with a dose of guilt, knowing that she and Zoe had something special, something that went beyond the casual flings of their pasts. She was honest, though, and shouldn't deny connections if she's correctly presented with opportunities. Lola, not knowing the existence of Zoe, to Sofia, proceeded to undress herself more and guided Sofia to pull off her underwear. Sofia went for what felt fun in the moment and told herself it was okay.

Back in Paris, Zoe was enjoying her night out with Fallon. They had wandered from the work event to a dimly lit cocktail bar, their conversation flowing easily. Fallon was charming and witty, her laughter infectious. Zoe found herself drawn to her, but her heart was anchored with Sofia. She excused herself to the restroom, pulling out her phone to send Sofia a quick message. "Paris is beautiful, but I wish you were here. I miss you."

Sofia woke up the next morning to the sound of her phone buzzing. She groggily checked her messages, her heart sinking as she read Zoe's words. She glanced at Lola, still asleep beside her, and felt a wave of nausea wash over her.

She quietly gathered her things and slipped out of the room, her mind racing with conflicting emotions. She knew Lola wouldn't take it personally to just leave without saying goodbye. Hooking up wasn't planned, and she was still processing the news that Lola had told her about her plan to move to Barcelona soon. So much rushing through her head.

She spent the day in a daze, her thoughts consumed by the night before. She felt guilty but also conflicted. She was single, after all, and she had every right to enjoy herself. But she also knew that she and Zoe had something special, something that went beyond their casual agreement. What was she doing? What does this mean? Why does it feel like a situationship all this sudden? She wondered if Zoe had slept with Fallon, if she, too, had been caught up in the moment. She has no idea what she was doing or how her night went since she hasn't reached out to her yet.

Their messages were minimal over the next day. Both women were consumed by their own thoughts and experiences. Sofia assumed Zoe probably noticed something was wrong with her distances and minimal communication. It wasn't until Zoe was back in Barcelona, her heart aching to see Sofia even though she could feel a gut feeling something wasn't right, that they finally agreed to meet up and talk.

As Zoe made her way to a random cafe, she felt a flutter of nerves in her stomach. She knew something was off, that Sofia had been distant since her night out with Lola. She took a deep breath, steeling herself for the conversation ahead. Whatever happened, she knew they needed to be honest with each other, to confront the ghosts of their past and present head-on.

Sofia was already waiting at the cafe, her long hair cascading down her back, her eyes filled with a mix of apprehension and relief. As Zoe approached, Sofia stood up, pulling her into a tight hug. They held each other for a long moment, the world around them fading away. Whatever happened next, they knew they had to face it together. But for now, they just held each other, their hearts beating in sync, their past and present lingering in the air around them like the elephant in the room. They sat down, and Sofia began to speak, her voice barely above a whisper. "Zoe, I need to tell you something..."

Chapter 27

Emotions of an affair that isn't an affair - Is this a situationship

———— ❤ ————

Sofia took a deep breath, her eyes locked onto Zoe's. She knew she had to be honest, no matter how painful it might be. "Zoe, I need to tell you something," she began, her voice steady despite the turmoil inside her. "Remember Lola, the friend I met up with while you were in Paris?"

Zoe nodded, her heart pounding in her chest. She had a feeling she knew where this was going, but she wasn't prepared for the wave of emotions that hit her. "Yes, I remember. I didn't know her name, but yes, go ahead."

Sofia looked down, her fingers tracing the pattern on the table. "We slept together, Zoe. It just happened, and I'm so sorry if this hurts you."

Zoe felt a pang in her heart, but she pushed it aside, focusing on the fact that they weren't committed. She was mad at herself for putting herself in this situation, for not guarding her heart better. "It's okay, Sofia. We weren't committed, and I understand. You are technically single, and you can do what you want," she said, her voice steady despite the turmoil inside her.

Sofia looked up, her eyes filled with a mix of relief and concern. "I'm so sorry, Zoe. I never meant to hurt you. But I need you to know that I'm not sorry I did it. I just didn't plan it, and it happened. I don't know why I felt guilty after. Again, I care about you, I'm sorry if it hurts you. That I'm sorry for."

Zoe nodded, her mind racing. She felt a rush of emotions—pain, anger, confusion—but she also felt a sense of understanding. She took a deep breath, ready to share her own truth. "I have something to tell you, too, Sofia. While I was in Paris, Fallon tried to kiss me. We kissed briefly. I wasn't into it, and I let her down easy and explained I was only interested in being friends."

Sofia's eyes widened in surprise, but she quickly regained her composure. "Thank you for telling me, Zoe. I appreciate your honesty. I knew it. I had a feeling about her. I could tell she was flirting. I don't blame her for trying. Paris is a romantic place, and you could have done anything you wanted. If you're into her at all, I would understand."

Zoe replied, "I'm sure nothing happened, and I didn't want it to. I know I'm free too; just wasn't interested."

Zoe felt a sense of relief. She knew they needed to be honest with each other, no matter how painful it was. "I just want to be honest with you, Sofia. I care about you, and I want us to have open communication. I'm not mad at you. I'm mad at myself for putting myself in this situation. I feel like I wasn't ready to have all these feelings and emotions shoved down my throat."

Sofia reached across the table, taking Zoe's hand in hers. "I care about you too, Zoe. And I want us to stay open. I think being honest with each other will only make us stronger, whatever we decide to do. I want to respect you."

As they sat there, their hands entwined, Zoe felt a sense of hope. Maybe this was a turning point, a chance for them to build something real and meaningful. But as Sofia began to speak again, Zoe felt a pang of unease.

"Zoe, there's something else I need to tell you," Sofia said, her voice hesitant. " There is a chance Lola would be moving to Barcelona. She might be here again, so I don't know how that will affect us."

Zoe felt a rush of emotions—confusion, fear, uncertainty. What did this mean for them? Would Lola's presence change things between her and Sofia? She took a deep breath, steeling herself for whatever was to come.

"What do you mean, Sofia?" Zoe asked, her voice steady despite the turmoil inside her. "How will her moving here affect us?"

Sofia sighed, her eyes filled with a mix of concern and determination. "I don't know, Zoe. I just know that I want to be honest with you, I did care about her once, maybe I could again. I am confused, maybe. I'm not sure how I feel about her yet and how I feel about seeing her again. I will let you know if she does move here. Just not sure what this all means and don't want to continue to hurt you."

Zoe nodded with a slightly forced smile.

Sofia's eyes widened in surprise. "You're not mad?"

Zoe sighed, running a hand through her hair. "I'm hurt, Sofia. Of course, I'm hurt a little bit. But I can't be mad at you. We're not committed to each other. We both knew something like this could happen." She paused, her mind racing with thoughts of their complicated situation. "I put myself in this position. I knew the risks, and I chose to be here anyway."

Sofia reached across the table, taking Zoe's hand in hers. "I'm so sorry, Zoe. I never wanted to hurt you. It just... happened. Lola and I have a history, and it was easy to fall back into old patterns."

Zoe nodded, understanding the complexity of Sofia's feelings. "I get it. And I appreciate your honesty. Let's give each other some space. See how things go."

Over the next few days, Zoe threw herself into her work and her new life in Barcelona. She spent time with her flatmates, Nicolas and Izzy, and her new friend Amos, exploring the city and trying to keep her mind off Sofia. She knew it would be hard, but she also knew it was necessary. They both needed time to heal and to figure out what they truly wanted.

Meanwhile, Sofia found herself torn between her feelings for Zoe and her wondering if she had lingering attachments to Lola. She spent her days working at the cafe, losing herself in the familiar rhythm of making coffee and chatting with customers. But her mind was never far from the complicated web of emotions she was trying to untangle. Will Lola move to Barcelona and start drama and jealousy and join this situationship further?

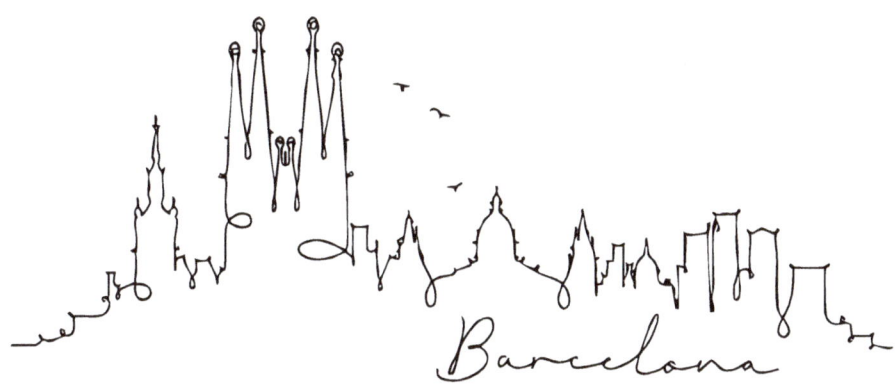

Chapter 28

Make-up sex for the win

——◦♥◦——

The sun rose over Barcelona, casting a golden hue across the city's vibrant streets. Zoe awoke to the sound of city transit buses beeping outside her window, a reminder of the life that pulsed around her. The warmth of the morning light filtered through the curtains, illuminating the room and chasing away the remnants of the night before. She turned to her side, expecting to see Sofia there, since before the weekend of what felt like cheating, they were almost inseparable, but instead, the space beside her was empty. A sting of disappointment hit her, but she quickly brushed it aside, reminding herself that their journey was still young and filled with potential.

After a quick shower, Zoe dressed in a comfortable pair of jeans and a soft sweater, ready to embrace the day. She made her way to the kitchen, making a cafe con leche de avena. The rich aroma filled the air, a comforting ritual that grounded her. As she sipped her latte, she couldn't help but think about Sofia.

Close by in the city, there was Sofia thinking of Zoe, more than she expected to. She started to think how she wanted to show her that she was more than just a casual fling. They had shared a connection that felt deeper than that, and Sofia was determined to nurture it.

Later that morning, Zoe received a text from Sofia: "Good morning, beautiful! Want to go for a ride later? I have a surprise for you. 😊"

Zoe's heart skipped a beat. The thought of riding with Sofia, feeling the wind in their hair as they zipped through the streets of Barcelona, filled her with excitement. It's like she instantly forgot the hurt and replaced it with excitement. "Absolutely! Can't wait! What's the surprise?" she replied, her fingers dancing across the screen.

Sofia's response came quickly: "You'll see! Meet me outside your place in an hour?"

Zoe finished her coffee and quickly gathered her things. The anticipation bubbled within her as she got ready for the day, her mind racing with possibilities. What could Sofia have planned? She hoped it would be something special, a moment that would solidify their growing bond.

When Zoe stepped outside the front door of her flat building she spotted Sofia standing at the corner with her long hair cascading over her shoulders and her smile radiant. Zoe felt a rush of affection as she approached, her heart swelling at the sight of the woman who had come to mean so much to her. "Gosh, why does this woman make me feel this way" Zoe whispered to herself.

"Hey, gorgeous!" Sofia greeted, her voice warm and inviting. "Ready for an adventure?"

Zoe grinned. "Siempre! What's the plan?"

Sofia leaned in, her eyes sparkling with mischief. "You'll see. Just trust me."

Sofia led Zoe to where her scooter was parked. Zoe's heart raced with excitement as she climbed on behind Sofia, wrapping her arms around her waist. The scooter roared to life, and they sped off into the bustling streets of Barcelona, the city unfolding before them like a vibrant tapestry.

As they rode, Zoe & Sofia felt freedom. The wind whipped through their hair, and the laughter they shared filled the air, a beautiful melody that resonated deep within them. They weaved through the streets, passing by colorful markets, stunning architecture, and the shimmering Mediterranean Sea. It was exhilarating, and Zoe couldn't help but feel alive in Sofia's presence.

After a short ride, Sofia pulled up to a picturesque park filled with blooming flowers and lush greenery. "Surprise!" she exclaimed, dismounting the scooter and helping Zoe off. "I thought we could have a picnic."

Zoe's heart fluttered at the thought. "This is perfect! You really went all out."

Sofia smiled, her cheeks slightly flushed. "I wanted to show you that you mean more to me than just a casual fling. You know you're more than someone I sleep with. I want to take the time to get to know you better."

Zoe felt a rush of warmth at Sofia's words. They spread out a blanket on the grass, and Sofia unpacked a basket filled with delicious treats—sandwiches, fresh fruit, vermouth, and pastries. They settled down, laughter bubbling between them as they shared stories.

As they enjoyed their picnic, Zoe felt a sense of comfort and safety enveloping her. They talked about their favorite music, where they grew up, their aspirations, and the little quirks that made them who they were. Zoe felt as though she was seeing a new side of Sofia, one that was open and vulnerable.

"Tell me about your family," Zoe asked, curiosity piqued.

Sofia's expression softened. "Well, most of my family is back in Argentina. I moved here to pursue more of my dreams, but I miss them every day. They don't really understand my choice to stay here, but I know it's what I need to do for myself. Luckily, I had my cousin here to start me out at the coffee shop."

Zoe nodded, understanding the weight of that decision. "It must be hard being away from them. I can relate; my family is back in the States, and I miss them too."

Sofia looked at Zoe, her gaze intense. "I'm glad we're both here, though. I feel like we create our own family, our own little world."

Zoe's heart smiled. "Yes, you are right, we do."

As the afternoon sun began to dip lower in the sky, casting a warm glow over the park, Zoe felt a spark of courage. "Can I kiss you?" she asked, her voice barely above a whisper.

Sofia's eyes lit up, and she nodded, her smile wide, happy she felt safe with her again. "Yes, please."

Zoe leaned in, their lips meeting softly at first and then deepening as they melted into each other. It was a kiss filled with promise, a beautiful affirmation of the connection they were building. The world around them faded away, leaving only the two of them in that moment.

But as they pulled away, the blissful atmosphere shifted. Sofia's phone buzzed in her pocket, pulling her back to reality.

Zoe glanced at the screen and felt her heart drop. It was a message from Lola.

"Hey, just checking in. Miss you! Can we talk?"

Sofia's stomach twisted with anxiety.

Zoe felt a surge of emotions—fear, jealousy, and confusion. Just when everything felt right, the specter of Lola loomed over them.

Sofia noticed her change in demeanor. "What's wrong?" she asked, concern etched on her face.

Zoe hesitated the weight of her thoughts pressing down on her. "It's just… it's Lola. She wants to talk."

Sofia's expression shifted, and Zoe could see the tension building. "Do you want to talk to her?" Zoe asked.

Sofia shook her head, frustration bubbling to the surface.

Zoe continues, "I can't help but think about how you didn't answer her call the other day when we were together. What if you still have feelings for her?"

Sofia's eyes widened, hurt flashing across her face. "Zoe, I didn't answer because I was with you. I thought we were having a moment."

Zoe felt a wave of guilt wash over her, but the fear was overwhelming. "I just don't want to be your toy. I don't want to be someone you're just using to fill time and be with whenever you want. Just to maybe be with someone else."

Sofia looked pained, and Zoe could see the internal struggle reflected in her eyes. "That's not fair. I'm trying to be honest with you, but it feels like you're not trusting me."

The tension escalated, and before long, they found themselves in a heated argument, emotions spilling over like a broken dam. They drank a lot of vermouth from the picnic basket, the alcohol only fueling their frustration and confusion.

"I just need to know if you would sleep with Lola again!" Zoe shouted, her voice trembling with emotion.

Sofia's expression crumpled, and tears filled her eyes. "How can you even ask me that? I care about you, Zoe. I'm trying to move forward, but it's hard when you keep bringing her up."

Zoe felt her heart break at the sight of Sofia's tears. "I'm sorry. I'm just scared. I don't want to lose this, but I feel like I'm competing with an ex-girlfriend, and I don't even know who she is or who she still is to you."

Sofia wiped her tears, her voice shaking. "You're not competing. I'm here with you. Can't you see that?"

Zoe took a deep breath, her heart heavy with regret. "I know. I'm just… I'm a mess right now. I don't want to make you feel bad for wanting to figure things out."

Sofia moved closer, wrapping her arms around Zoe, and they both cried together, the tension slowly dissipating in the embrace. "I don't want to hurt you," Sofia whispered.

"I don't want to hurt you either," Zoe replied, her voice muffled against Sofia's shoulder. "I'm sorry for being so emotional. I just need time to process everything."

Sofia held Zoe tightly, and in that moment, they found solace in each other, the weight of their fears slowly lifting. They spent the night talking, sharing their vulnerabilities and insecurities, and by the time they fell asleep in each other's arms, they felt a renewed sense of connection.

The next morning, Zoe awoke to the soft light filtering through the curtains and the gentle warmth of Sofia beside her. She turned to see Sofia still asleep, her features relaxed and peaceful. Zoe felt a surge of affection, grateful for the bond they were building despite the challenges.

After a few moments, Sofia stirred, her eyes fluttering open. A smile spread across her face as she met Zoe's gaze. "Good morning, beautiful," she murmured, stretching out beside her.

"Good morning," Zoe replied, feeling a spark of joy at the sight of Sofia. "Last night was intense, huh?"

Sofia chuckled softly. "Yeah, but I think we needed it. I want to be open with you, Zoe. You mean a lot to me."

Zoe's heart swelled at Sofia's words. "You mean a lot to me too. I promise to work on my insecurities. I just want to be the best version of myself I can be."

Sofia leaned in, brushing her lips against Zoe's in a soft kiss that sent shivers down her spine. The kiss deepened, and Zoe felt a rush of warmth enveloping them. Sofia asked Zoe, "Is this okay? Can I have you again? Right here…" as Sofia starts to kiss Zoe's stomach and then up to her breast while lifting up her shirt. Zoe exhales and softly replies, "Yes, amor, please, I want you."

Sofia takes off Zoe's clothes piece by piece. Kisses her body along the way. She stays on her neck for a while and starts to move her hair back while kissing her neck and shoulders. Zoe starts to undress Sofia as well and then starts to touch her back and then inner thighs until Sofia opens her legs up, slowly pushing Zoe's hand and fingers closer to her pussy. "Please, baby, go in, I miss you." As Zoe goes inside Sofia with her two fingers, they both start to moan in synced pleasure. They both have been craving this feeling again, this closeness.

Suddenly, Sofia throws Zoe up on the balcony window and goes deep inside her. Making sure that she feels wanted and satisfied. Zoe reaches around to touch Sofia as much as she can, too, her ass and her vagina as well, trying to hold herself up against the window and pushing Sofia into her more. As they start to moan more and more, they fall back into bed. Feeling so into each other and about to orgasm at the same time.

After a long intimate sexcapade, they pulled away, both breathless. "I should get going," Sofia said reluctantly, glancing at the clock. "I have work at the cafe."

"Right, of course," Zoe replied, feeling a twinge of disappointment at the thought of Sofia leaving. "But can we do this again soon? I want to keep exploring what we have."

Sofia smiled, her eyes shining with warmth. "Definitely. I'd love that. I'll be dreaming of you all day."

As Sofia gathered her things, Zoe felt a sense of hope blossoming within her. They had faced their fears and vulnerabilities, and while the road ahead might be rocky, they were willing to navigate it together.

After Sofia left, Zoe took a moment to collect her thoughts. She felt the weight of the previous night's emotions still lingering, but she also felt a sense of clarity. She would embrace the uncertainty, knowing that love and connection could blossom even amidst the chaos.

Later that day, Sofia finally checked the voicemail from Lola. Her mind raced as she pressed play, the familiar voice echoing in her head. "Hey, Sofia. I just wanted to let you know that I'm not moving to Barcelona after all. I've decided to stay in New York. I hope we can talk soon."

Sofia felt a mixture of relief and confusion wash over her. Perhaps this was a turning point, a chance for her and Zoe to truly explore what they had without the shadow of Lola looming over them. With a deep breath, she decided to focus on the present, ready to embrace whatever came next in her journey with Zoe.

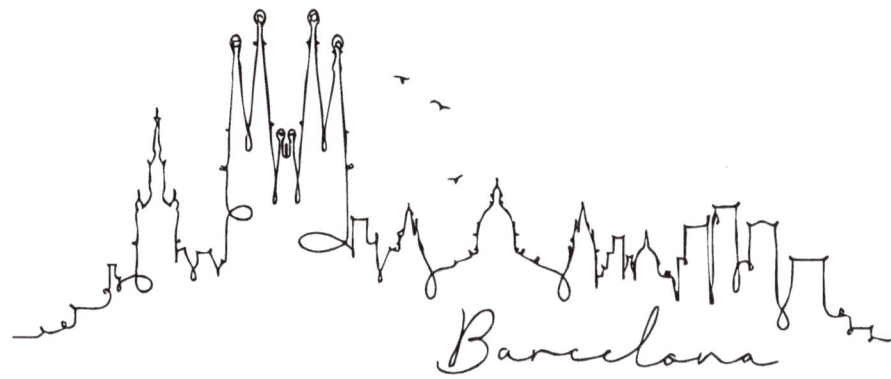

Chapter 29

Not afraid to fall

───♡♥♡───

Z oe sat on the balcony outside her bedroom, the Barcelona sun casting a golden hue over the city. The vibrant streets below were alive with the sounds of laughter and music, but her heart felt heavy with uncertainty. She had spent the past few days thinking about her life, but the weight of her feelings for Sofia and the recent revelations about Lola lingered in her mind like a storm cloud.

As she sipped her coffee, Zoe's phone buzzed with a message from Sofia. "Hey, can we meet up? I have something important to tell you." Zoe's stomach twisted with anticipation. She knew this conversation was coming, and she felt a mix of excitement and dread.

"Sure! How about the coffee spot we love?" Zoe replied, her fingers trembling slightly as she hit send.

The response came quickly. "Perfect. See you soon."

As Zoe made her way to the cafe, her mind raced with possibilities. What could Sofia possibly want to discuss? Was it about Lola? About their relationship? She took a deep breath, trying to calm her nerves. Whatever it was, she knew they needed to talk.

When she arrived at the coffee shop, she spotted Sofia sitting at a table, her long hair cascading over her shoulders, her expression serious. Zoe's heart raced as she approached, her stomach twisting with anxiety. "Hey," she said softly, taking a seat across from Sofia.

"Hey," Sofia replied, her voice steady but filled with emotion. "I've been thinking a lot about us, about everything."

Zoe felt a rush of anticipation. "Me too. I want to be honest with you about how I feel."

Sofia nodded, her gaze unwavering. "I appreciate that. I've been thinking about what you said before about wanting to take things slow. I want to be open with you, but I also need to be honest about where I'm at."

Zoe's heart raced as she listened, trying to read Sofia's expression. "Okay, I'm listening."

Sofia took a deep breath, her eyes searching Zoe's face. "I care about you, Zoe. I really do. But I also have a lot going on in my life right now. I just got out of a complicated situation with Neila, and I'm not sure if I'm ready to jump into something serious again. I want to focus on my work, my life here, and figuring out who I am without the past weighing me down."

Zoe kinda felt this coming & she also understood Sofia's perspective. "I get it. I don't want to rush you into anything you're not ready for. However, I also don't want to be just a casual fling. I want to build something real with you if I was to live here, ya know?."

Sofia's expression softened, and she reached across the table to take Zoe's hand. "I want that too, Zoe. But I need time. I want to be sure of what I want before I commit to anything."

Zoe felt a mix of relief and frustration. "I respect that, Sofia. However, eventually I need to know where we stand. I don't want to be in limbo when I get to that point where it feels like we should progress or move on. So if I do come back again, like we talked about, I might not be able to keep doing this."

Sofia nodded, her eyes filled with understanding. "I know. And I'm sorry if I've put you in that position. I just need to figure things out for myself first. I don't want to hurt you, and I don't want to lead you on. You deserve more than that."

Zoe took a deep breath, her heart heavy with the weight of their conversation. "I understand. I just wish things were simpler. I am about to make some big decisions again, and I might move back sooner than you think. I'm not sure I can come live here and keep seeing you and give you the same time and capacity of romantic space in my life if you're not ready for anything further than this style of whatever this is. "

Sofia smiled softly, her eyes filled with warmth. "Me too, Zoe. But life isn't always simple. We're both figuring things out, and I want to be honest with you about where I'm at. Thank you for telling me where you are with this, too. I do want to see you, and you're right. You will need to decide as well."

As they sat in silence, Zoe felt a rush of emotions—fear, uncertainty, and a flicker of hope. She knew they had something special, something worth exploring, but she also understood the importance of giving each other space to grow.

"Okay," Zoe said finally, her voice steady. "I'm willing to give you the time you need. I think I need this time too to give us time apart, to see how we really feel. If we feel good about it. I need to know if this is worth pursuing… before I move on, be single or put myself out there and move on with someone else who is more ready."

Sofia nodded, her expression serious. "I understand, and I appreciate your honesty. I'll keep you updated on how I'm feeling. I want this to work, Zoe. I really do. I like you a lot. For the record, Lola is not moving here. I wouldn't want you to be worrying about someone I don't care about in that way. I wanted to tell you. I would want you to feel important and I am not afraid to commit. Just not sure it's the right time for me to give you the best version of myself till I have more time."

Zoe smiled and expressed softly. "I hope this conversation didn't ruin my last few couple weeks with you. Can we just enjoy each other and live in the moment, like we do best? I adore you."

"Absolutely," Sofia responded.

As they finished their coffee, Zoe felt a sense of peace wash over her. They were both on the same page, ready to navigate the complexities of their relationship together. She knew it wouldn't be easy, but she was willing to put in the effort.

Zoe and Sofia spent more time together, exploring the city and deepening their connection. They visited beautiful parks, enjoyed romantic dinners, and spent lazy afternoons wrapped in each other's arms. Each moment felt precious, a reminder of the bond they were building.

Days later, the weight of their unspoken feelings lingered in the air. Zoe couldn't shake the sense of urgency building within her. She wanted to know where they stood, to understand if they were moving forward or if they were destined to remain in this uncertain space.

One evening, as they sat on the balcony of Zoe's flat, the sun setting behind them, Sofia decided it was time to confront her feelings. "Zoe, can we talk? I'm feeling a lot right now ?" she asked, her voice steady but filled with emotion. "Yes, baby, of course. What is it?" Zoe says as Sofia grabs her hands and guides her to the bed. They are now lying down and staring into each other's eyes deeply.

Sofia asks Zoe, "Can I just have you here for the night and at this moment, look at me." as she intensely kept the stare into her eyes. "Yes, love, I'm here," Zoe says, then kisses Sofia. Sofia then turns her head to the side of Zoe's face and, puts her lips to Zoe's ears, and whispers, "I'm not going to be afraid, I'm sure, baby…" She kisses softly and continues, "I'm falling for you…" Zoe hears this, and it sends shivers and tingles all down her body, her heart beating fast, filled with love and joy, and she feels like she's melting into Sofia.

Zoe carefully and gently, with her soft, sexy voice, says, "You are not alone.." she kisses her back on her ear, then continues and says the magic words:

"I'm falling for you too…"

That moment was only theirs: an intense and passionate love-making, beyond *just sex* kinda moment they shared. A kind they could never forget.

Chapter 30

Zoe's Birthday & Goodbyes

———♥———

oe is in her cozy flat. It was a week before she was set to leave, and the weight of impending separation hung in the air like a thick fog. Yet, amidst the bittersweet emotions, there was an undeniable spark of excitement. Zoe and Sofia had spent the last few days deepening their connection, sharing dreams, and planning for Zoe's return. It felt as if they were weaving a tapestry of love, each thread representing a moment they cherished together.

Zoe sat at her small kitchen table, sipping her afternoon coffee while Sofia was gone at work. She glanced at her phone, her heart racing as she read a message from Sofia: "Come downstairs and grab a jacket? I have some exciting news!"

Zoe's heart fluttered at the thought of seeing Sofia. She quickly finished her coffee, threw on a denim jacket, and headed out the door, the warm breeze welcoming her as she stepped onto the street.

When Zoe spotted Sofia at the street corner, her long hair cascading over her shoulders, a radiant smile lighting up her face. Zoe felt a rush of affection as she approached, and Sofia stood there next to her scooter to greet her with a warm embrace & kiss.

"Hey, beautiful," Zoe said, her voice soft.

"Hey! I have some incredible news," Sofia replied, her eyes sparkling with enthusiasm and holding out her extra scooter helmet for Zoe. "I found a few apartments for you to check out when you come back! I think you'll love them. Hop on."

Zoe's heart swelled at the thought of having a place to call her own in Barcelona. "Really? That's amazing! I can't believe we're actually making plans for my return."

Sofia nodded, her expression earnest. "I want you to feel at home here, Zoe. This city has so much to offer, and I want to be a part of that adventure with you, anything I can do to help."

As they chatted over croissants & cafe con leche avena, Zoe felt a sense of hope wash over her. They discussed potential apartments and neighborhoods, their voices filled with excitement as they imagined what life could be like when Zoe returned. The thought of starting her studies in Spanish and immersing herself in the culture thrilled her. It felt like a new chapter was beginning, one filled with promise and adventure.

"Zoe," Sofia said softly, breaking the comfortable silence. "I've been thinking a lot about us and what it means to be apart. I want to make this work, but it's going to take effort from both of us. It's only a couple months, right?"Zoe turned to Sofia, her heart racing. "I want that too. I know it won't be easy, but I believe in what we have. Let's just say several weeks."

Zoe nodded, feeling a sense of determination. "And I'll be studying Spanish, which will help me integrate more into your world. I'll save as much money as possible. It's something to look forward to, right?

"Exactly," Sofia replied, her voice filled with warmth. "We can do this. I believe in us."

As they shared a tender kiss, Zoe felt tingles all over her body. The connection they had was undeniable, and she was ready to embrace the challenges ahead. They spent the rest of the evening wrapped in each other's arms, falling deeper as the stars twinkled above them.

In the days that followed, Zoe and Sofia dove into preparations for her return. Zoe registered for a student visa and enrolled in Spanish classes at the local university. The excitement of starting a new chapter fueled her determination. Meanwhile, Sofia worked hard at the cafe, saving money for their future adventures together. They talked about traveling to other parts of Europe they had been dreaming of and ideas like renting out Zoe's new apartment while they traveled to minimize costs.

Their days were filled with laughter, late-night talks, and passionate moments that left them breathless.

As the week progressed, Zoe began to feel the weight of goodbyes looming. She knew that their friends—Nicholas, Izzy, and Amos—were planning something special for her birthday, which was just around the corner. The thought of celebrating with her friends brought a sense of joy, but the reality of leaving weighed heavily on her heart.

One evening, as they sat on the balcony of Zoe's flat, watching the city lights flicker to life, Sofia turned to her, her expression serious. "Zoe, we need to talk about the goodbye party. I want to make it special for you, but I also want to know how you're feeling about everything."

Zoe sighed, her heart heavy. "I'm excited for the party, but I can't help but feel anxious about leaving. I know we've made plans, but the thought of being apart is really hard."

Sofia reached for Zoe's hand, squeezing it gently. "I know it's tough. But think of it as a temporary separation. We're building something beautiful together, and this is just the beginning. You'll be back soon."

Zoe nodded, tears stinging her eyes. "I want to believe that. I really do. It's just hard to imagine being away from you. I can't believe you are choosing this life with me, too. I know it's scary and going to be hard on us both for a bit."

Sofia leaned in, her forehead resting against Zoe's. "We'll make this work. I promise. And when you come back, it'll be like no time has passed. We'll have so many adventures waiting for us. I am glad I have you in my life."

In the days leading up to the party, Zoe and Sofia threw themselves into preparations. They picked out decorations, planned the menu, and invited their friends. The excitement of the celebration provided a welcome distraction from the impending goodbye.

On the night of the party, Zoe's flat was filled with laughter and love. Friends gathered, filling the space with warmth and joy. Nicholas, Izzy, and Amos had gone all out, transforming the flat into a vibrant celebration of Zoe's life in Barcelona. Colorful streamers hung from the ceiling, and fairy lights twinkled, creating a magical atmosphere.

As the evening progressed, Zoe felt overwhelmed with gratitude for the people in her life. They shared stories, toasted to new beginnings, and celebrated the love that had blossomed between Zoe and Sofia. The energy in the room was infectious, and Zoe couldn't help but feel a sense of belonging.

When it was time for cake, Zoe stood in front of her friends, her heart swelling with love. "Thank you all for being here and for making this night so special. I'm so grateful for each of you. You've made my time in Barcelona unforgettable."

As they sang "Happy Birthday," Zoe felt tears prick in her eyes. She glanced at Sofia, who was beaming with pride and love. In that moment, Zoe knew that no matter the distance, their connection would remain strong.

Later in the evening, as the party began to wind down, Zoe and Sofia stepped out onto the balcony, the cool night air wrapping around them. They stood in silence for a moment, taking in the view of the city that had become their playground.

"Zoe," Sofia said softly, breaking the quiet. "I want you to know that no matter what happens, I'm here for you. We're in this together."

Zoe turned to Sofia, her heart full. "Te quiero, Sofia. I'm so grateful for everything we've shared. I can't wait to come back and continue this journey with you."

Sofia smiled, her eyes glistening with emotion. "Te quiero yo tobien, Zoe. We'll make it through this. We are so worth it."

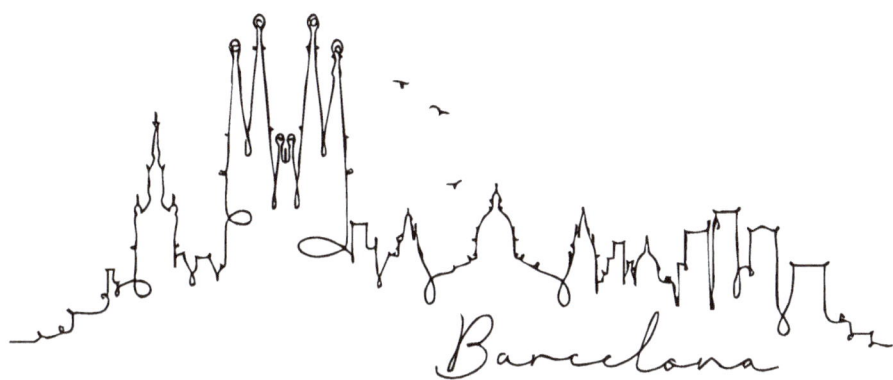

Chapter 31

Te quiero mucho - I'll miss you!

———❤———

Zoe stood at the curb, her heart racing as she watched the unmistakable glow of the sunset bathe the streets of Barcelona in a warm golden hue. She clutched her suitcase tightly, the weight of her emotions almost too much to bear. The Uber was on its way, and she could feel the gravity of the moment settling over her like a heavy blanket.

Sofia stood beside her, tears glistening in her eyes as she fought to maintain her composure. The air between them was thick with unspoken words and lingering feelings, the reality of their impending separation hitting them both like a tidal wave.

"I can't believe this is happening," Zoe said, her voice trembling as she fought back tears. "It feels so surreal."

Sofia reached for Zoe's hand, squeezing it tightly. "I know. I'm going to miss you so much. It feels like we just started to figure things out."

Zoe nodded, her heart aching at the thought of leaving Sofia behind. "I promise I'll call you every day. Time will fly by, and before we know it, I'll be back in Barcelona."

Sofia smiled, though it didn't quite reach her eyes. "I hope so. Just promise me you'll take care of yourself while you're gone."

Zoe swallowed hard, tears spilling down her cheeks. "I will. I promise." She leaned in, pulling Sofia into a tight embrace, their bodies fitting together perfectly. It felt like a moment suspended in time, a bittersweet farewell that neither of them wanted to end.

As they pulled away, Zoe looked into Sofia's eyes, searching for reassurance. "I'll always cherish the time we spent together," she said softly. "You mean so much to me."

Sofia's voice cracked as she replied, "You mean so much to me too, Zoe. I don't want this to be the end of us."

Just then, the Uber pulled up, and Zoe's heart sank. She glanced back at Sofia, her chest tightening with emotion. "I guess this is it," she said, her voice barely above a whisper.

"Not for long," Sofia said, her eyes filled with determination. "We'll make it work. Just remember that I'm here for you, no matter what."

Zoe nodded, her heart aching as she stepped back to grab her suitcase. "I'll see you soon, okay?"

Sofia nodded, tears spilling down her cheeks as she stepped forward, pulling Zoe into another embrace. Their lips met in a desperate kiss, filled with longing and promises of what was to come. As they pulled apart, Zoe felt a rush of warmth, a reminder of the connection they had forged.

"Te quiero mucho," Zoe whispered, her voice thick with emotion.

"Te quiero yo también," Sofia replied, her eyes glistening with unshed tears.

Zoe took a step back, her heart racing as she climbed into the backseat of the Uber. She glanced back at Sofia, who stood there, tears streaming down her cheeks. Sofia then walked to her scooter and was about to put her helmet on, afraid to watch her Uber drive away. Zoe told her driver to stop as she jumped out of the car, ran towards Sofia, and latched her arms around her one last time. Kissed her again and then ran back into the backseat of the Uber as she rolled down the window. "I'll miss you!" she shouted, her voice filled with emotion.

"I'll miss you too!" Sofia called back, waving as the car pulled away.

*… to be continued with Zoe in Barcelona. The New Year
- Part 2*

"forgive me every time i kiss you like that...

i want it to always feel like the last, so when i see you again, can feel like the first" - Necool

"No puedo un-love carino"

About the Author

Originally from San Diego, Necool is a traveler, poet, and storyteller with a deep passion for writing. What she adores the most is her friends, family and her dog. She loves coffee, photography and almost always has music playing in the background as if there is a soundtrack of her life. With a heart full of wanderlust, she finds inspiration in the beauty of everyday moments, crafting stories that celebrate love and the art of romanticizing life. Through her writing, she explores not only identity but the magic of human connection, inviting readers to embrace the world with wonder and an open heart. ♥

www.ingramcontent.com/pod-product-compliance
Lightning Source LLC
Chambersburg PA
CBHW051205120626
46547CB00013B/1217